Making Everyday Choices

Making Everyday Choices

Helping Students in Grades 2–5 Practice the Art of Thinking

Lin Josephson

ROWMAN & LITTLEFIELD
Lanham • Boulder • New York • London

Published by Rowman & Littlefield
An imprint of The Rowman & Littlefield Publishing Group, Inc.
4501 Forbes Boulevard, Suite 200, Lanham, Maryland 20706
https://rowman.com

Unit A, Whitacre Mews, 26-34 Stannary Street, London SE11 4AB, United Kingdom

Copyright © 2018 by Lin Josephson

All rights reserved. No part of this book may be reproduced in any form or by any electronic or mechanical means, including information storage and retrieval systems, without written permission from the publisher, except by a reviewer who may quote passages in a review.

British Library Cataloguing in Publication Information Available

Library of Congress Cataloging-in-Publication Data

Names: Josephson, Lin, author.
Title: Making everyday choices : helping students in grades 2-5 practice the art of thinking / Lin Josephson.
Description: Lanham, Maryland : Rowman & Littlefield, [2018]
Identifiers: LCCN 2018008805 (print) | LCCN 2018025374 (ebook) | ISBN 9781475840810 (Electronic) | ISBN 9781475840797 (cloth : alk. paper) | ISBN 9781475840803 (pbk. : alk. paper)
Subjects: LCSH: Thought and thinking--Study and teaching (Elementary) | Decision-making--Study and teaching (Elementary)
Classification: LCC LB1590.3 (ebook) | LCC LB1590.3 .J67 2018 (print) | DDC 370.15/2--dc23
LC record available at https://lccn.loc.gov/2018008805

This book is dedicated to my grandson, Riley, and my granddaughter, Reese, who teach me more than I could ever teach them. They are the loves of my life . . . and the thinkers of the future.

Contents

Preface: Why?	xi
Acknowledgments: Thank You	xiii
Introduction: How?	xv
1 Dos and Don'ts	1
2 One Step Ahead	5
Buy Now . . . Uh Oh . . .	5
No Time?	7
Simplify	9
The Dreaded Homework	11
Tipping the Scales	13
3 Action Figures	15
"No Thanks"	15
Which Way?	17
Rain, Rain, Rain	19
Sick to Your Stomach	20
Adults Make Decisions, Too	21
4 Opinion Lab	25
Back It Up	26
The Majority Rules	27
Open Minds	29
Fill in the Blanks	31
Should I or Shouldn't I?	33
Honest Opinion?	34
5 Streamlining	37

Stuff	37
Write About "Anything"	40
Too Many Library Books!	41
Recipe For Friendship	42
Mixed Up	45
Zeroing In	46
Pick a Number, Any Number!	48

6 Side by Side — 51
- Meet The Inventors — 52
- Gorilla or Elephant? — 53
- Juggling Act — 55
- Six Words — 56
- Me, Me, and Me — 57
- What's In a Name? — 58
- Take Me to Your Leader — 60
- Who Says I'm Bossy? — 62

7 Don't Jump! — 65
- Is Seeing Believing? — 65
- Scrumptious! — 67
- Fair or Unfair? — 68
- How Does Your Garden Grow? — 69
- Race in the Park — 71
- What's Inside? — 72

8 Huh? What Did You Say? — 75
- Better Safe than Sorry — 75
- The Early Bird Gets the Worm — 77
- Don't Bite Off More than You Can Chew — 78
- Don't Count Your Chickens Before They Hatch — 80
- Haste Makes Waste — 82
- Two Heads Are Better than One — 83

9 How Did This Happen? — 87
- Oh, That Little Voice — 87
- Walking the Dog — 89
- Who Did It? — 91
- We Can — 92
- You Never Know — 94
- Imagine If . . . — 96
- Cause and No Effect — 98

10 Words of Wisdom: From the Experts — 101
- Make It Safe . . . Relatable . . . Open . . . — 101
- Going Beyond . . . Taking Risks . . . Making Choices . . . Making Mistakes . . . — 102

Construction Paper . . . Oxygen . . . Philosophy . . .	104
Expectations . . . Routines . . . Accountability . . .	106
Scenarios . . . History Lesson . . . Good Planning . . .	107
Consequences . . . Prompts . . . Dialogue . . .	108
Intervening . . . Rethinking . . . Knowing When . . .	110
Role Modeling . . . Connecting . . . Visualizing . . .	111
Reaping the Rewards . . . Celebrating . . . Building Confidence . . .	113

11 Food for Thought: A Menu for Educators 117
    Leave It Alone 117
    Outside the Cocoon 118
    In My Opinion 118
    What Do I Really Think? 119
    Counterproductive 120
    Getting Full 121
    Wrong Foot Forward 121
    Cut It Down 122
    Who Me? 122
    Before It Spirals 122

About the Author 125

Preface

Why?

Henry Ford said, "Thinking is the hardest work there is, which is probably the reason why so few engage in it." He was right.

While Ford's decades-old proclamation is humorous on the surface, the meaning behind it is serious and is severely relevant in today's world. Any educator who has ever heard a student say "I can't think!" or "I can't decide!" is not alone.

The *why* of this book is simple: to have children step back and carve out some time from their chock-full everyday lives and receive the much-needed chance to practice their own thinking—thinking that may even be considered old fashioned but is increasingly necessary for them to become self-reliant thinkers who can make their own decisions.

The vehicles that spur this thinking and decision making along are conduits or prompts that will help turn your classroom into a thinking laboratory—a forum where your students can practice thinking in a carefree, relaxed atmosphere, without the angst or frustration many kids feel when they must figure something out or sort through choices and make decisions.

However, the goal of getting your kids to think goes beyond your classroom walls. The intention is that your students will be able to take the essence of something they've learned from a prompt and adapt it, stretch it, and use it to help them solve a problem of their own or make a tough decision.

As much as these exercises will give your students a chance to think, they will also give you a front row seat to see why students make the decisions they do and use the thought processes they do.

For every prompt that is offered, the students are encouraged to explain their decisions and their thinking. Through these discussions and the sharing of ideas, students will realize that many of them face the same types of quandaries. They can see how their peers would attack certain problems and situations and get advice on why a particular way is the better choice.

The ensuing discussions and analysis of choices, as well as guidance from the author and you, will give the students some necessary tools they can use when they have to rely on themselves to make clear, level-headed decisions.

As a first-grade teacher and a philosophy for children practitioner for second graders, I've seen the amazing results that can occur when we let kids think for themselves and figure things out. Even when things don't go as planned, some valuable knowledge can be learned.

Better thinkers become better doers.

Acknowledgments

Thank You

With infinite gratitude, I'd like to thank my husband, Sandy, our sons, Alex and Dan, and our daughters-in-law, Rebecca and Yi Ying, whose neverending support and encouragement gave me the confidence to write this book.

An extra dose of thanks goes to Dan, for his sage educational insight, and, to Alex, for his expert social media help. I am grateful to Ramona Sojacy and Debby Richardson for their helpful consulting, to Sue and Harry Friggle, Mary Greenberg, Pam and Dennis Swanson, and Andrea and Pete Wilkens for their continued interest in the manuscript, and to Cynthia Vengraitis for her long-ago encouragement to become a teacher.

I'd like to thank all the incredible educators who contributed to the "Words of Wisdom" chapter (chapter 10) for sharing their expertise and for their dedication to their students.

More thanks to Drs. Joe Oyler and Maughn Gregory for being such wonderful mentors at Montclair State University and to Jenn Esposito at South Mountain Elementary School for being so open minded and generously welcoming me into her amazing classroom to teach philosophy to her second graders.

For the kids at Far Brook and South Mountain, thanks for immeasurably enriching my life and warming my heart.

And much gratitude to the Rowman & Littlefield team of Tom Koerner, Emily Tuttle, and Chris Fischer for their help and guidance.

Another note of appreciation goes to Sandy for not only being my astute editor but also for being my patient partner in life and for everything he's done while I wrote this book, including making his spinach artichoke pasta.

Introduction

How?

Before we tackle the question of "How can we help children think?" we have to look at thinking as one more category of life that requires practicing.

With this in mind, the conduits or prompts in this book will act as catalysts to give your students opportunities to have practice runs with their thinking and decision making and help them gain confidence in these skills so they can become more self-reliant and self-assured thinkers . . . and doers.

The prompts are formatted as brief stories, exercises, poems, and activities. They are kid centered to make your students feel comfortable and mimic some of the everyday challenges and decisions kids have to make. They are designed to spark your students to think in sensible yet creative ways to figure things out, make level-headed decisions, and solve problems.

Whether the exercises revolve around silly questions like "Would you rather bathe a gorilla or take an elephant for a walk?" or practical ones like "What's the best way to express your opinion?," the prompts are intended to make your students think hard and make choices.

Emphasize to your students that these exercises are not tests. They are similar to the practice sessions they would have to play a sport or a musical instrument or to do anything else that requires time and effort to improve.

The prompts run the gamut from those that offer option answers to those that are open ended without any suggested answers. They are divided into eight categories: planning and thinking ahead; taking action; expressing opinions; narrowing down choices and getting organized; collaborating and teamwork; making assumptions and jumping to conclusions; idioms; and cause and effect.

Always ask your students, "Are there other good decisions or choices that haven't been included or we haven't discussed?" "Did we miss something?"

The format and structure of this book hinges on the prompts being presented by the educator in a casual, stress-free atmosphere, with peer discussion and educator guidance. Setting aside time for these discussions is at the core of this thinking laboratory. It is during this time that your students can analyze and defend their own thinking.

Asking children to explain their choices can let them see the arc of their thinking. This, in turn, can often help them realize where their thinking is clear and level headed and why it has resulted in a good decision. Conversely, it can also show them where their thinking breaks down and why it results in a poor decision.

The discussion time also gives the students a chance to learn from their peers or to teach them something. It is also an opportunity for you to pose your own questions and those provided by the author to expand the students' thinking. Guidance and suggestions by the author are also included to explain why certain choices or options make more sense than others or why some decisions are better than the rest.

While the author's input is intended to help you clarify the rationale behind some of the choices, it is imperative that the students always explain their reasoning first so they are not influenced by someone else's thinking.

There are introductory directions and guidelines for every prompt. The prompts are meant to be universal, but feel free to change settings, wording, or whatever is needed to help you tailor them to expressly meet your students' needs.

It is recommended that your students always have paper and writing utensils when they are doing their thinking. Some kids think better this way, and it can always be helpful to jot something down or even sketch it out.

If a prompt requires more than paper and pencil, it will be noted within the instructions. There are also times when "chart paper" is used as a generic term for a visual aide to display any information that the class needs to see. You can use a chalkboard, dry erase board, Smart Board, or any other handy methods.

By presenting these prompts, you also have another opportunity to reinforce some of the concepts you use in teaching everyday academic subjects: to underscore the importance of listening and reading carefully.

Some of the conduits are specifically designated as "collaborative efforts" in which the students will be divided into small groups to do their thinking. However, if you feel other conduits would lend themselves to collaborative efforts for your students, please convert them.

Hopefully, you and your students will view the time spent with this book as similar to the time engaged playing games that sharpen their math, language arts, or science skills.

No doubt, you know how much your students enjoy hearing stories about your life and maybe even your childhood. Some of the prompts are especially conducive to story sharing, but you can use any of them to make further connections with your students.

With you as their model, your students will see that when they must make a choice, a decision, or think about something independently, they can do it without freezing up or giving up.

Let your students know that thinking, like life, is a journey.

Help them enjoy the ride.

Chapter One

Dos and Don'ts

As educators, we strive to have our students become published authors, fluent readers, accurate mathematicians, and knowledgeable scientists.

As any inspiring teacher knows, academic subjects are but one aspect of the classroom experience that educators impart to their students. Another crucial element in this equation is guiding children to become self-reliant, resourceful, creative problem solvers who think sensibly and make prudent decisions on their own.

This is indeed a tall order, but helping guide this process along is one essential ingredient: confidence. Your confidence in your students and their confidence in themselves and their own decision-making abilities will help them become the thinkers and doers they have the potential to be.

This chapter offers dos and don'ts to help foster the self-reliance and sensible thinking skills every kid needs. Some ideas might seem obvious, but somehow, throughout the course of a jam-packed, stimulating rollercoaster ride of a day, they can get lost in the shuffle, popping up at that split second before your head hits the pillow, when you say, "Gee, I could have done . . ."

DO let your students know:

- You understand that thinking takes time and is hard work.
- Even adults have trouble making decisions.
- They're not alone in having to make decisions all day long. Other kids do it too, and sometimes they, too, are puzzled by what they should do.
- Everyone makes mistakes. What's important is figuring out how to fix them, change them, and learn from them.
- You think they are capable of making the decisions they're being asked to make.

- Every time they make decisions, they are practicing their thinking.
- When a problem arises that your students should be able to solve themselves, remind them that every problem demands questions such as "What if . . . ?" "How could I . . . ?" "When should I . . . ?" Let them see that asking themselves questions about how to solve a problem can help them think sensibly and make their decisions on their own.
- There are times when the adults are in charge, no matter how much children feel the decision should be up to them.

DO ask your students:

- To set a pause button in their thinking and ask "Does this make sense?"
- To ask themselves "Is this decision practical?"
- To ask themselves "Can I make a better choice?"
- What they would say to a friend if a friend arrived at this decision or thought a certain way.
- Why an ill-conceived decision or action was not prudent. Let the children think this out so they can see what went wrong and why. Let them lead the conversation; you can follow.
- For their input to help solve classroom problems: "How can we solve this? How can we fix that?" Make sure that their thinking is backed up with good reasons and facts. Knowing that their decisions will affect them and their classmates will help boost their confidence.
- For their opinions on just about anything you think is relative and age appropriate. "Do you like the weather we're having today?" is an innocuous question, but it can give students another chance to think and voice their opinions in a casual, nonthreatening atmosphere.
- For their input to help you solve problems. They'll love helping you and will feel important.

DO remind your students:

- Good thinkers think about the consequences, both good and bad, that a decision will have.
- Good thinkers use the word "because" to help them back up the reasons for their thinking. "I'm doing it this way because . . ." Getting children accustomed to using "because" not only helps them explain the reasons for their personal decisions and problem solving but is also beneficial for a multitude of academic situations: "I like this book because . . ." "I know that this math answer is correct because . . ." "Because" helps move their thinking forward and into a deeper, more qualifying place.
- Every experience, good and bad, is a learning one.

DO:

- Point out their successes.
- Remember that some kids are so afraid of making a mistake that they don't want the responsibility of making a wrong decision. In their minds, no decision is better than a wrong one. They may need more encouragement than others to make choices on their own.
- Step back: Give the children time to think on their own about how to solve a problem and make their decisions.
- Step in when you see that the tipping point toward frustration is on its way.
- Encourage your students to control their first impulses and think an idea and decision through.
- Notice things that some kids are struggling with in the classroom and ask other kids for advice. If, for example, some children, particularly younger ones, have difficulties arranging their backpacks, you can say, "I know sometimes packing up a backpack can be a hard thing to do. Does anyone have some good suggestions about how to make it easier to do that?"
- Take time every day to ask the students which decisions they made as a class that were particularly great and which ones could have been better and why. You can add your own thoughts, but let the kids do their assessments first.
- Think about establishing a "Think Tank" in your classroom, sort of like a suggestion box where kids can write down problems they need help solving.
- Role model your own decision making, letting your students see how you make choices, why you eliminate some, and keep others. The more that kids see that everyone has to make decisions and choices every day (even the family dog decides whether to sleep on the couch or chair), the more relaxed they can become about making their own choices. Watching you will help them almost by osmosis.
- Let your students daydream, if only for a few minutes a day. This is a great time for kids to free up their minds and let them wander. Amazing thinking can happen!

DON'T:

- Rush in to help a child the second she or he can't fix or do something on his or her own.
- Constantly do things for your students they can do for themselves in an effort to keep the classroom running efficiently and humming.
- Let a student's poor decision or thinking become the talk of the classroom.

- Forget that kids are individuals. Some will let imprudent decisions and thinking roll off of them, while others will think a mistake is the end of the world. Don't let that happen.
- Let your students think they can never ask anyone for advice. Some children take everything an adult says literally, so an interpretation of being "independent" and doing things on their own can be misunderstood as "Never ask for help." Explain the difference between getting helpful advice or suggestions and having someone else do their thinking for them. However, remind your students that when they make a decision, they are accountable for that decision, no matter who may have advised them.

Chapter Two

One Step Ahead

Childhood is full of "living in the moment," which is how it should be. So trying to go against that by instilling the merits of planning and thinking ahead into children's decision-making DNA requires time, diligence, and patience.

Yet by constructing a game plan and thinking things through with step-by-step scenarios, children can better analyze their alternatives, weigh the pros and cons, craft good decisions, and avert poor ones. A little contemplation ahead of time can smooth some of the rough edges around making decisions and create a more relaxed atmosphere about making them.

BUY NOW . . . UH OH . . .

Money management, like time management, is a crucial responsibility and decision-making category that takes practice. It's not uncommon for college students to be clueless about how to manage their finances. Maybe a little practice and awareness years ahead of time could lead to more confident, financially astute young adults down the road.

This riddle is a teaser to a story about money management. As you read it, stop every few sentences and ask the students if they know the answer yet. They might think they know it from the first line, but the more you read, the more they may realize those first guesses aren't right.

In a subtle way, this teaches your students that gathering more information about something allows them to discard certain choices in favor of better ones. Let the kids shout out their answers as you go along (chaos inducing but fun) or reflect silently on what they think it is until the end.

I am something that can be here today and gone tomorrow. You can save me . . . or not.

You can lose me. You can find me. Some people say you can never have enough of me. Some people waste me. Some people use me for good. I can be new. Or old.

You will have to work for me. Sometimes people give me away. You can trade me for things. I am very well known no matter where I go. I have different names in different countries. I come in different shapes and sizes. Sometimes I have pictures of famous people on me. In the United States, I am paper and metal. When I am metal, sometimes people flip me to help them make decisions.

What am I? Money! (You can ask your students which hint made them realize it was about money.)

This conduit involves a magical genie . . . but a realistic quandary:

A genie comes up to you and gives you a lot of money as a gift. He says you have six days to use the money to buy anything you want! On the seventh day, he'll appear again, and he promises that if you have any money left, he'll give you more money to spend for another six days. He'll keep giving you money as long as you don't spend it all before he visits you again.

What good luck! You buy gifts for your family, your friends, and yourself. You donate money to a charity to help other people. You buy clothes. You donate money to an animal shelter. It is the fourth day, and you still have some money left!

Then you see an incredible toy at the store. You have to have it. The clerk tells you that it's the last one left and someone else might buy it if you don't. But if you buy it, you'll spend every last cent.

The genie's proposition sets up a money dilemma that plagues everyone: "Should I be practical or impulsive?"

Before you present these two options, tell your students they should select the *wisest* plan for the future:

A. Buy the toy now and spend all your money.
B. Walk away from the toy and keep the money you have left.

For the students who argue that *Option A, "Buy the toy now and spend all your money,"* is the best decision for the future, what are their reasons?

- Does having the toy now help plan for the future? If so, how?
- Is the temptation of getting the toy immediately stronger than planning for the future?
- Are their reasons based more on emotion than practicality?
- Do some kids want to buy the toy now because they're assuming (guessing) it will be gone if they wait until the genie gives them more money?

How do the students who selected the most sensible choice, *Option B, "Walk away from the toy and keep the money you have left,"* explain their thinking?

Does it make more sense to give up one toy to have more money for the future? Would it be hard to walk away?

Did some students choose Option B because they assumed the toy would still be at the store (or another store) after they received more genie money? Explain that while they chose the wisest plan for the future, their thinking was based on a guess or an assumption without any facts backing it up.

Some students might say they chose Option B even though they knew they could miss out on having the toy. Maybe without even realizing it, these students thought the hardest because they went forward with a calculated risk, which is a mature, sophisticated way of thinking.

When you describe Option B, in addition to using words like practical and responsible, slip in rational and logical too. Getting kids familiar with these words can help them categorize their choices. Even second graders can understand them if you say they mean the same thing as "making the most sense."

It's too bad that in real life, nobody has a genie. But asking your students to make a decision between being practical and being reckless might crack open the door to discussions about money and the best ways to manage it.

You can end the discussion with these questions:

- "Are you being responsible to yourself if you think about how you should spend money?"
- "If you have money, is it ever okay to buy whatever you feel like?"
- "Did you ever spend money on something and then wish you hadn't?"
- "If you have money, should you save it? If yes, what should you save it for? If no, why not?"

NO TIME?

Time management is difficult for anyone to master, let alone kids whose definition of time can be defined by doing something when they want to do it.

Teaching children the concept of planning to do a task or chore when they have the time to do it rather than waiting until the last minute to get it done can be challenging. Time management is all about making choices and decisions. See what your students say about this example:

On a certain Saturday, you'll be allowed to go to the movies with your mom as long as you clean your room by 3:00. "No problem!" you tell yourself. You think you have plenty of time to do it because you have nothing else to do this day. You'll clean your room later. So you visit a friend, watch TV, ride your bike, play with your dog, and read a book for a long time.

But the one thing you haven't done is clean your room. Before you know it, it's 3:00. When your mom sees your messy room, she asks, "Why didn't you clean your room?" And you say, "I ran out of time to do it." You miss going to the movies because now you have to stay home and clean your room.

Open a dialogue by asking the students, "Did you really run out of time to clean your room?" If some students feel that, yes, time did run out, ask them to explain why and how the time ran out.

Does anyone say that there was enough time to clean the room? What makes them say that? Should the room have been cleaned first, before anything else was done?

One key to time management is taking stock of what is the most important thing that needs to get done and when. A way to help children become attuned to prioritizing is by explaining that a time-sensitive situation or responsibility should take top priority.

Relate the questions back to this prompt and ask:

- "Did you have to ride your bike by a certain time?"
- "Did you have to clean your room by a certain time?"
- "What was the most important activity that had to get done that day?"

Help your students see that a deadline—and there will be numerous deadlines of various forms throughout their lives—pushes something to the top of the list.

Here are a few questions you can ask your students to promote some thinking about their own time management:

- "Did you ever think that you had 'all the time in the world' and then you ran out of time to get something done? What happened?"
- "Which choices can you make to better plan your time?"
- "Do you think that you ever waste your time? If so, how do you waste time? Was there a better way to use that time instead of wasting it?"

Look for answers that reflect an awareness that we can't stop time from slipping away, but we can control our behavior toward it. Two ways to do that are by prioritizing and using up "free" time to accomplish something that we know must get done.

This strategy is simple to model in the classroom: "Since we have some extra time now, let's make the covers for your stories because we know that tomorrow will be super busy, and we won't have time to do it before the authors' party."

As always, a story of your own time mismanagement, preferably a humorous one, will have an eager audience.

Another tool to help kids become better at managing time is fostering the habit of estimating how much time it will take to do something. Even children who are not yet adept at telling time can use barometers to help them: Will it take as long as watching a TV show? As long as we spend on a math lesson? As long as the time you have for lunch at school?

You can also experiment with this in the classroom. Think of something specific you or the kids do every day—something as simple as coming into the room in the morning and getting everyone settled in or a walk to the library.

Ask the kids how long they think these tasks will take (with younger students you can use barometers: as long as counting to 100 two times, etc.), and then time them. You can have the class practice time estimations every now and then by asking, randomly, "How long do we think this will take us/you to do this?" Even if estimates are off, an awareness of how much time it will take to do something can help your students hone their time management skills.

SIMPLIFY

Needed: Chart paper.

This experiment will help your students engage in a little forethought and planning so they can think more clearly when decision-making time arrives. This can be especially beneficial to kids if they know ahead of time that they'll be faced with making an ultimate decision quickly.

Arrange ten to twenty (the higher number for older students) library books on a table or on the floor. Choose books from different genres and separate them according to those genres.

For younger students, you may want to keep the number of genres to a minimum. Display some books that are below the reading level of your least proficient readers and some that would be extremely beyond the comprehension of your most advanced readers.

Present this prompt as an experiment to your students: You want them, in lickety-split time, to choose a book they would like to read in the future. Encourage them to make a note of the book they want for an upcoming library visit.

On the chart, write down the genres or book categories you've selected: fiction, nonfiction, science fiction, and so on. You might want to include some books written by authors your class is especially fond of or books that cover topics that interest many of your students.

Divide the students into groups of three to five children. Tell them that before they look at the books, you want them to study the book categories and decide which *one* genre they will choose a book from.

They will have two minutes to share with their group which categories they want. Then they'll have two more minutes to look through the books when it is their turn at the table. Remind your students to keep the books in their categories at the display table.

For the purposes of this experiment, explain that you want the students to stick with the category they chose. Emphasize that all the students should get a chance to look at every book in their category; so to be fair, no one should monopolize any one book.

While the other students wait for their turns, they can have a free chat time or a task to work on so they won't get too antsy.

As each group finishes perusing the books, have the students discuss why they chose their particular books within their groups. Tell them to be specific in their explanations and go beyond "I just liked it."

Visit each group as the children discuss their choices, asking such questions as, "Did you read this author before?" "Are fiction books your favorite kind of reading?" Ask them any other questions that might spark them into explaining why they made a decision to choose one book over another.

Also probe a little further: "Did you avoid certain books?" "Why?" This might prompt the explanation that some books didn't make the cut because they were too easy, too hard, or uninteresting. Let your students see that reasons for not choosing something are just as important as reasons for choosing something.

After the students have shared their book selections within their groups, come together as a class and pose these questions:

- "Was it hard to choose a book in two minutes? Why/why not?"
- "Was it easier or harder to make a decision about one book because you already knew which category you wanted ahead of time? Why/why not?"
- "Did knowing the book category ahead of time help you to take less time or more time to choose your book? Why/why not?"

For those students who found it helpful to think ahead, ask them if thinking and planning ahead could help them with other decisions in their lives. If so, how?

For those students who didn't feel that thinking ahead was helpful, ask them for ideas that could have helped them. They just might come up with constructive and productive solutions everyone could use.

If they could have changed their category, do the students think that it would have taken them longer to make a decision? Shorten it? If some students didn't make a decision, ask them why they couldn't decide. What could help them make a decision like this the next time?

When the discussion is done, explain to the class that the experiment they worked on was to see whether a little planning and thinking ahead could help them make quick decisions. Do they think it was a successful or unsuccessful experiment?

THE DREADED HOMEWORK

Educators know that no other word elicits more groans and moans from school-age children than "homework."

While controversies and divergent opinions swirl around the efficacy and merits of this eight-letter word, teachers still hand out homework assignments and students still do them. (Well, most students still do them.)

You've probably explained your homework policy at the beginning of the year to your students and their guardians. However, with all the other things that must be accomplished in a single day, the topic of homework is often relegated to giving out assignments and not actually discussing the ins and outs of the process of doing homework.

By presenting this prompt, you can illustrate how planning and making one decision can help your students do their homework more efficiently and with less frustration.

You have three homework assignments in one night. One assignment is your favorite subject, and you think it will take the least amount of time. The second assignment isn't hard to do, but it will take you a little longer to finish than the first assignment. The third assignment is a subject that is hard for you, and you know it will take you the most time to get it done.

Which assignment should you do first?

A. The easiest one
B. The hardest one
C. The medium one
D. Do a little bit of each one until they are all done.

Option B, "The hardest one," is the most practical choice. By putting the hardest assignment at the top of the list, your students will reap the benefits of having the most focus and energy for their most arduous task. As the clock ticks toward bedtime, fatigue and boredom can set in, making it harder to concentrate and focus.

To make an analogy, pose this question: "Let's say you're exhausted. Which would you rather do: run around the school three times or do two jumping jacks?"

Most students will choose the jumping jacks. Explain that this is similar to doing harder homework first. They will be "fresher" if they tackle the most difficult assignment when they are at their sharpest.

Students who chose *Option A, "The easiest one,"* are not alone. Doing the "easiest" homework is often the most popular choice. Sometimes the easiest assignment gets done first because it's seen as the most fun: If someone likes to draw, then having to draw a map of their home state could be their favorite assignment of the night and the one that gets top priority.

Nevertheless, these "easy" assignments can sap time and energy from your students as they start over multiple times to perfect a map of New Jersey. Then, all of a sudden, it's bedtime, and nothing else has been started, much less completed.

Sometimes students choose the easiest assignment because it gives them a sense of accomplishment—something they can cross off their list.

But that feeling of accomplishment can also be felt by completing the most taxing assignments first. Show your students that they can divide the difficult homework into chunks: "Okay, now I've done the first four questions, or Part 1 is done . . ." so they can feel and see their progress.

Sometimes choosing to do the easier assignment first is a way to procrastinate and avoid doing the hardest assignment. Explain that procrastinating comes with its own set of negative effects: "Sometimes the longer we wait to do something—whether it's homework or something else we don't want to do—the more we don't want to do it. Sometimes we make it more awful in our minds than it really is."

Some kids may have chosen *Option C, "The medium one,"* because they think it is a compromise. After you hear the students' rationales for this choice, explain that, even though it is "medium," this kind of assignment will still take up some of the concentration, motivation, and energy that would be best directed to the hardest assignment first.

Besides, after doing the hardest assignment, the kids can breathe a sigh of relief.

Option D, "Do a little bit of each one until they are all done," might not make any sense to adults, but it can be appealing to children because they can bounce between easy, medium, and hard. Ask them, "Would you stop playing baseball in the middle of a game to play tennis, and then go back to the baseball game?" They might say that would be crazy, but ask them why it would be crazy. See if their reasons include variations of breaking their concentration, losing their focus, and/or being distracted.

Also ask your students about the physical logistics tied to alternating subjects: "Do you need to switch books? Writing utensils? Papers?" All of this is time consuming and wastes time that could be spent doing something more appealing than homework.

After your students have discussed their choices, ask them the following questions, reminding them to be specific:

- "What makes homework easy?"
- "What makes homework hard?"
- "What makes something take a long time to do?"

- "What makes something take a short time to do?"
- "Is homework ever fun?"
- "What makes homework fun?"

Defining the different levels of homework can help your students categorize and classify their own assignments and help you glean some insights into their homework habits. Your students' descriptions might also enable you to better construct homework assignments or help you to improve your directions and instructions.

From time to time, you can ask the class how it would rate the previous night's homework, what order the assignments were done in, and why they were done in that order.

These questions can serve as intermittent reminders to your students to prioritize their homework assignments so they can work more efficiently. As the year goes on, your students' responses to these occasional questions may continue to give you a heightened understanding of their homework habits.

TIPPING THE SCALES

Needed: Prepared in advance a three-column chart labeled "Choice," "Pros," "Cons," or any other words that would connote the meanings of pros and cons.

Making a decision is a multifaceted process that's composed of many factors. One effective way to deconstruct this process and break it down into manageable, kid-sized chunks is by teaching children to compile lists of the pros and cons for each of their choices.

However, to maximize the usefulness of this tool, the "weight" of each pro and con on the list must be assessed. This helps students qualify each positive and negative and avoid the natural temptation to make a certain decision because it has the most number of pros or the least number of cons.

While this approach can help result in solid, judicious decisions, it is only productive if the pros and cons are accurate and "true." If children already have a preconceived decision in their heads—even without knowing it—they can skew their pros and cons to bend toward that decision, which may not be the best one.

Before you present the prompt, describe a quick definition for *pro* and *con*. In basic terms, a *pro* is a reason to do something and a *con* is a reason not to do something. Instead of *pro* and *con* you can use *plus* or *minus, good* or *bad, positive* or *negative,* or *yes* or *no*.

Tell the students to pretend that your class has won a contest and they have to decide which prize would be best for the entire school:

A. Get more books for the library

B. Add more technology—this can be more computers, more educational programs/games (or the introduction of technology into your school), and so on.
C. Add more art supplies (or the introduction of them)
D. Provide candy every day for all the kids and teachers

Begin by asking the students if they have other prizes in mind that would be useful. After any choices have been added, ask the kids to describe the pros and cons for each choice and to make sure that each one is accurate and "true."

Listing pros and cons is a great visual for kids, but impress upon the students that what's important is the "weight" of those pros and cons, not how many there are of each. Explain that some pro reasons might be *more* positive than others and therefore *weigh more*; some con reasons might be *more* negative than others and *weigh more*.

When the students justify their reasons for a pro or a con, they can use a one to ten scale (ten being the best positive reason and the worst negative reason) to help them evaluate their "weight."

This kind of analytical thinking requires kids to think deeply and hard, but it is worthwhile to spend time and effort on.

If some students chose *Option D, "Provide candy every day for all the kids and teachers,"* hear them out—they might have some interesting pros and cons. Could there possibly be anything bad about having a daily candy treat?

Once the pros and cons have been listed and weighed, ask the students to vote for which prize they want to give to their school. When all the choices are tallied up, ask:

- "How did you decide on that prize?"
- "Did you base your decision by counting up the pros and cons?"
- "Did any pro 'weigh' so much that it made you choose that prize?"
- "Did any con 'weigh' so much that it made you not want to choose that prize?"

If you still have time, try this little fantasy with the kids and see what they come up with: "Here are two more prizes you can choose between: a trip on a rocket ship to Mars for all the students in the school or a day at a dinosaur park that has real-life dinosaurs."

While these are imaginary options, have the kids weigh the pros and cons in a realistic manner: Would a trip to Mars take too long? Would it be too cold? How would the dinosaurs react to humans? Would being with actual dinosaurs give the students a chance to do some real-life research?

Chapter Three

Action Figures

One of the biggest frustrations kids have is that they can sometimes feel helpless—even if, on the surface, they might be content to let others take over for them.

It may be easier and less time consuming if someone else constantly saves the day, but this doesn't pave the way for kids to set their own course of action—it paves over it.

The prompts in this section will help students see that they can make a difference in their own lives when they choose to act instead of sitting idly by or waiting for another person to do something for them. The aim is to let children realize they will have many opportunities in which the actions they take, even as kids, can positively impact their lives.

Show them that they are not powerless . . . but that they are powerful.

"NO THANKS"

Classrooms are a microcosm of society, replete with different personalities and temperaments. As educators, you help your students thrive and be confident and comfortable in their own skin. Yet in an effort to let them become everything they want to be and everything they can be, you encourage them to take actions that will move them out of those zones they find so comfy and cozy.

Some children expend much time, energy, and effort on almost everything they do. Other students are acutely aware of how "easy" most things are for them. And some kids are especially adept or talented in certain areas.

No matter which types of students you teach, there are bound to be some children who are always reluctant to try something new or immediately want to stop doing something when they don't excel.

There are two phrases that kids often define themselves by: "I'm really good at this" and "I'm not really good at that." Often kids who are used to sailing through most things or excelling in certain areas get stuck in their comfort zones and are afraid to venture into new territories because they think they will "fail."

Other times children shun new activities because doing something challenging makes them nervous and uncomfortable. And sometimes some children eye a new venture as one more thing they won't be good at.

This conduit can begin a discussion that will help your hesitant students see that making a decision to try something new or challenging can be enriching, interesting, and fun.

Begin by telling this story:

George is nine years old and likes to draw. George's drawings are amazing, and he knows that he wants to be an artist when he grows up.

The only thing George ever wants to do is draw. When someone asks him to do something else or to try doing something different—even playing a new game with his friends—George says, "No thanks."

One day, one of George's friends asks him, "Why do you always say 'No thanks' to everything except drawing?" George answers, "Because I'm not good at anything else."

Is this the best way for George to act?

- A. No, this is not the best way for George to act. He should try new things.
- B. Yes, this is the best way. If George knows what he likes, he should only do what he likes.

To help George blossom and thrive, we hope that he would choose *Option A, "No, this is not the best way for George to act. He should try new things."* When your students defend their reasons for selecting Option A, does anyone mention that by trying something new, George could discover an activity that he enjoys and wants to continue doing? You could ask, "Can you enjoy doing something even if you are not really good at it?"

Some students, particularly older ones, might argue the opposite: They could try something new and have an awful time. (They might be the same students who chose Option B as George's best choice.) Ask them, "What makes something an awful experience?" (Note if anyone responds "Not being good at it.")

Not-so-great experiences can be learning ones and can give your students a chance to be proud of themselves for trying something new and challenging. Tell your class that practicing doing hard things or new things while they are kids will give them skills that will help them face other challenges when they are older—maybe even next week when they are seven days older.

Many of your students may think that the better choice is the "safest" one,

Option B, "Yes, this is the best way. If George knows what he likes, he should only do what he likes."

For the students who chose Option B, ask:

- "How is it good for George if he only does one thing?"
- "If George doesn't try something new, how will he ever know whether or not he will like anything else?"
- "Drawing was once something new to George. What if he never tried it?"
- "Do you think that George might lose his friends because they want to do other fun things and all he wants to do is draw?"

Explain to your students that it is certainly okay not to like something after you give it a chance. But let your students see that avoiding something new and different because they're afraid they won't be good at it is a sure way to miss out on a lot of interesting experiences and fun times.

To relate this conduit back to your academic curriculum, make an analogy to your students' reading experiences. You can ask them, "Do you remember when you first learned how to read?" Even second graders who are not yet proficient readers will relate to this question.

Let your students describe the books they read and liked when they were brand new readers. Ask them, "Would you still want to read only those books?" See if they can articulate the path they took, gradually reading more complex books until they acquired the reading skills they have now. Then ask, "Would you like to stop practicing reading and read the kinds of books you're reading now forever?"

It is a good bet that most students, if not all, will say that they want to acquire higher and broader skills so they can read and understand harder, more interesting books as they get older. Drawing a parallel between choosing to stretch their reading skills and saying "Yes" to other new experiences might help your students see the merits of leaving their comfort zones behind and trying to do things they are "not really good at."

WHICH WAY?

As adults, starting a new job can be exciting as well as nerve wracking. Children can experience those same emotions when they start a new school, no matter how old they are. One of the biggest worries kids have about a new place is getting lost. Happily, this is one concern that kids can put to rest by planning and taking their own actions.

Begin the prompt with this story:

You are excited to be in a new school. You are looking forward to making new friends and learning a lot. However, there is something troubling you.

No matter how hard you try, you get lost whenever you have to go to the bathroom, the library, the nurse, or anywhere in the school by yourself.

Ask the students, "Is there anything you can do?"

    A. No, you just have to get used to getting lost.
    B. Until you know where everything is, carry a piece of paper and pencil with you when you walk through the school alone. Write down notes about where certain places are or sketch them out.
    C. Make sure you don't ever have to go anywhere in the school by yourself.

While it may seem like a lot of work to some kids, *Option B, "Until you know where everything is, carry a piece of paper and pencil with you when you walk through the school alone. Write down notes about where certain places are or sketch them out,"* is the best solution.

By choosing this option, your students become their own problem solvers by making a decision to help them improve a situation they don't like. They are making a plan and taking action instead of becoming continually frustrated and upset by a common situation that anyone can experience.

Sometimes "go with the flow" is a good choice to make, but it's not a viable option when something difficult for a child can be fixed or changed. *Option A, "No, you just have to get used to getting lost,"* doesn't provide any solution to this problem and only prolongs the upset and frustration. What rationale did the students have for choosing this option? After they've explained their reasoning, you can ask, "Which way makes more sense? To try to fix a problem or to continue being upset by it?"

When your students discuss their reasons for choosing *Option C, "Make sure you don't ever have to go anywhere in the school by yourself,"* ask them, "Is it realistic that you'll never have to use the bathroom, or go to the cafeteria, library, or any other place in the school by yourself?" After thinking about it some more, can they tell that this is an illogical and impractical decision?

Options A and C are choices of inaction. Try using this simple gesture to model to your students how performing one action can transform a problem into a solution.

Situate yourself into an obviously uncomfortable position in a chair. Tell the kids, "Boy, am I uncomfortable," and complain for about thirty seconds. Then say, "I don't know what to do. Does anyone have any ideas?"

Because kids love giving their teachers advice, you will undoubtedly receive many suggestions, with the majority of them along the lines of "Just change your position!"

Once you do and become comfortable again, you can sow the seeds of an idea by simply saying, "Wow, there was something I could do to help myself instead of being uncomfortable and complaining."

No need to say anything else. Let them think about this.

RAIN, RAIN, RAIN

Have your students imagine that today is the end of the year picnic. But on this day, a bit of bad luck arrives: a big thunderstorm is raining down, soaking everything and flashing lightning everywhere. This means there won't be any freeze tag or any games that could have been played outside. Tell your class that you would understand if they felt a little bummed out and disappointed.

Then ask, "What is the best decision we could make to save the day?"

A. Mope around the classroom and hope the rain stops.
B. Try to convince your teacher that you should still be able to have the picnic outside.
C. Make a different kind of picnic with indoor games and activities.

Option C, "Make a different kind of picnic with indoor games and activities," is the only option that allows the students to still have fun and salvage the day. This option allows the children to take the situation into their own hands and change its unfortunate dynamic.

Option C may seem like an obvious solution to adults, but it requires changing thinking gears. For some kids, when something doesn't match up with the way they pictured it, moving forward can be difficult. You can point out that while the picture may not be the same, there will *still* be fun. The fun will be different, but there will be fun!

If anyone chose *Option A, "Mope around the classroom and hope the rain stops,"* ask how they thought this could save the day. Sometimes adults, too, want to mope around when things don't go our way. A little, "Oh, man, it's raining, and we can't have our picnic outside" is fine, but prolonged sulking is not productive.

Explain to your students that they will be wasting their time by feeling sorry for themselves instead of making the most of the day and having fun. You might add that "hoping" for something means not taking any action, and without actions, nothing happens.

The class picnic only comes around once a year. Ask them, "When you go to bed at night, would you rather be thinking of all the fun you had or how disappointed and sad you were?"

The students who chose *Option B, "Try to convince your teacher that you should still be able to have the picnic outside,"* might view themselves as leaders looking for a solution. While it might be admirable to want to engage in dialogue with their teacher and save the picnic, this is a good time to talk about safety first and how safety should be a consideration in every decision your students make.

If you want to extend this scenario, spend a few minutes asking your students to create some games and activities they could do if this really happened to them. See what they come up with, always keeping an eye out for creativity and practicality.

SICK TO YOUR STOMACH

The anticipation bubbling up inside kids as they await an exciting event in their lives knows no bounds. When something threatens to get in the way of that good time, however, any iota of level-headed thinking can get pushed aside . . . and prudent decisions don't stand a chance.

The situation portrayed here might be familiar to your students, as well as to any adults in your school. Trying to decide whether logic or emotion should win out can be disconcerting for anyone.

You've been waiting to go your best friend's birthday party for weeks. You're so excited you can't stand it. Now that the day has arrived, you're counting the hours until it's party time! It's going to be awesome!

Uh oh . . . About an hour before the party, something happens. You start to get the chills and feel like you're going to throw up. Your head hurts and you feel achy all over. The flu? A virus? Maybe you ate too many licorice sticks last night?

You decide it can't be the licorice sticks. You know you're sick. You don't want to say anything to anybody in your house because they'll take your temperature and make you drink hot tea and lie down in bed. And then they'll say, "Party? So sorry, honey, but you can't go to the party. You're sick. I know you feel awful about missing it, but, really, you can't go. Really, really sorry."

You've got the whole conversation mapped out in your head. When they say this, you'll say, "I have to go! It's my best friend's party! I have to be there!" You'll make sure that every sentence ends in an exclamation point! But you know you're doomed. If you say you feel sick, they'll make you stay home.

You look in the mirror. Whew—you don't look sick, and you're not coughing, well, at least not yet anyway. You could perform your best acting job and pretend nothing is wrong. You look at the clock—fifty-eight minutes to go before the party starts. It won't be hard to stay out of your family's way until then. Lay low until it's time to go. A perfect idea! You're sure you can pull it off!

After you've read the story, ask the class, "If this were you, what would be the best decision to make?"

A. Tell the adults in your house that you feel sick and stay home.

B. Pretend you are not sick and go to the party.

With only two decisions, it shouldn't take your students long to decide whether or not they should attend the party. *Option A, "Tell the adults in your house that you feel sick and stay home,"* is the most sensible choice and the one that adults would want a child to choose.

By choosing Option A, your students are choosing to act now and possibly avoid a worse situation later. When the students defend their choice of Option A, does anyone mention that this option is the most "responsible" one?

Without making an assumption, do any of the students think that it is possible they *could* feel sicker at the party? Do they imagine what it would be like if they threw up in the middle of eating birthday cake?

Even if they don't anticipate getting worse, do the students think they would feel so sick that they'd be miserable at the party and not have a good time? Does anyone say that by attending the party, they could infect other kids with whatever they have?

Many people, adults included, would be guilty of implementing *Option B, "Pretend you are not sick and go to the party."* Why did the students think this was the best decision to make? Do they know "for sure" they'll magically feel better when they arrive at the party? Is that an assumption? Is it realistic?

Kids who chose this option may emphatically believe that feeling sick at the party would still be better than staying home.

When all the reasoning is done, ask the class, "Has anything like this ever happened to any of you?" You can also share your own story.

ADULTS MAKE DECISIONS, TOO

Needed: Copies of the questionnaire, "I DECIDED...," which is embedded within this conduit. Each student will bring the questionnaire home and have it filled out by one adult in the household. Chart paper to record students' responses.

While children often become frustrated by the decisions and choices they have to make, they can take for granted or be oblivious to the fact that the adults in their households make numerous decisions every day and act on them—just like their teachers.

This thinking conduit is in three parts and will take two sessions to complete. The first and last parts will be done in the classroom and the middle portion will be done at home by the students' guardians.

Open a dialogue by asking, "Do you think the adults in your house make decisions every day?"

Once it's established that yes, indeed, the adults in their homes make myriad daily decisions, ask your students, "What kinds of decisions do you think they make?" See if they can be specific and cite examples of what the adults might have to decide. Write down their responses on the chart for a discussion that will take place after you receive the guardians' answers.

For the middle part of the prompt, please make copies of the section below so each student can give one to an adult in the household.

"I DECIDED . . . "

One decision I made today was

_____

_____

_____

(Your decision can be as simple as deciding what to eat for breakfast.)

How did you decide on the choice you made?

_____

_____

_____

(Please be as specific as you can about why you made this choice or took this action. For example: Was your decision based on a practical matter? Did you decide to do something today because there was a deadline? Did you make your choice because it was something you wanted to do or liked to do? Did you decide to do something because you knew it would help someone else?)

If possible, on the day you receive the guardians' responses, have your students share their adults' decisions. Can your students detect any patterns in the adults' choices? Were decisions based on practical matters, such as going food shopping? Were some decisions emotional ones, like watching a favorite TV show because it made someone relax or laugh?

Did it seem as if some decisions were difficult choices for the adults to make? Were there any similarities or differences between the decisions the students thought the adults might have to decide and the actual decisions made by the adults?

After you discuss the adults' decisions, ask the class, "What is one decision you made so far today? How did you make that decision?"

Do the students see any similarities or differences between the decisions they make and how they make them and the adults' decision making? Are there any similarities or differences between their personal decision making and the way decisions are made in the classroom?

Let your students see that decisions, no matter how big or small or who makes them, require a thought process and taking action.

Chapter Four

Opinion Lab

With their unfiltered dispositions, children can say the most thought-provoking comments while dispatching an earful of honest talk to anyone who will listen.

However, things can become complicated for kids when they're asked, "What is your opinion?" At the core of every opinion is a decision or a choice. Expressing an opinion connotes a more personal sharing than yelling out the spelling of a certain word—it means taking a stand in front of others.

Some kids relish the spotlight, gladly giving their opinions, confidently and unabashedly staking their claims, and exclaiming what they think, even if theirs is the lone voice of dissention.

There are other children who half-heartedly raise their hands, implying that they are not sure what they think. And there are children who are so reticent to voice their opinions that they'll hide behind the person in front of them or do anything to avoid making a public declaration of what they think—especially if they feel they are out of step with the general consensus.

Some children nervously look around to see how their friends are responding, blindly going along with them. If a friend raises his or her hand to favor Choice #1, then so will these children. Sometimes an overwhelming number of children feel the same way about something, and this is reason enough to have some kids say they feel that way too . . . even if they don't.

When children are expressing their opinions, remind them that *because* is a good thinker's best friend. While asserting an opinion is not the same as shouting out a math fact, it still has to be well thought out and backed up by good, solid reasoning. Facts, evidence, and examples help shore up an opinion.

Remind the kids, "When people ask for *your* opinion, that means they want to know what you are thinking and what's going on in your brain. If you just go along with someone else's opinion, those thoughts come from that person's brain, not yours. Is your brain in somebody else's head?"

BACK IT UP

Needed: One sheet of paper with three pictures printed on it for every group of two students. A list of suggested pictures follows.

The goal for this conduit is to encourage kids to become more comfortable saying what they believe and think and to give good reasons for their opinions. It will be the catalyst for a discussion on how important it is for kids to express their own opinions and refrain from agreeing with others solely because they are friends, more popular, or because they can't make up their own minds.

Download from the internet or clip art any pictures or photos that your students would relate to and organize them into classifications. For example: colored rocks, seashells, stickers, pencils, baubles, toys, games, animals, places to visit, backpacks, artwork, photographs of kids doing different activities, such as playing baseball, reading, going on a fossil hunt, and so on.

For every team of two students, you'll need three pictures on one sheet of paper. Headline the paper with one question: "Which animal looks the most interesting to you and why?" "Which game would you like to play and why?" "Which activity would you love to do and why?" "If you could buy one of these items, which one would it be and why?"

(It would be best to have different picture sheets for each group so the kids won't hear what their peers are saying, but if you're pressed for time and it's easier, distribute the same picture sheet to all the groups.)

After you divide the students into their teams, explain to them: "Look carefully at the pictures and think about the question at the top of the paper. When you have your answer, share your opinion with your partner, and then your partner will share his or her opinion with you."

Emphasize to the students that they must have good, specific reasons for choosing what they did. For example:

1. "I don't know why, but I like the Lego toy the most."
2. "I like this Lego toy the most because I like designing buildings, and I can do that with Legos."

Ask your students, "Which sentence helps you better understand why this person liked the Lego toy the most?"

When all the sharing is done, pose these questions:

- "Did anyone have a different opinion from your partner's?"

- "Did anyone agree with your partner?"
- "Did you have the same reasons for agreeing?"
- "Did you have different reasons for agreeing on the same thing?"

Then ask:

- "Did you agree with your partner because you wanted to go along with him or her?"
- "Did you give the same reasons as your partner for choosing something because it was the easiest way to think?"
- "Did you agree with your partner because you like him or her?"

After your discussion, you can extend your students' thinking with these additional questions:

- "When someone asks for *your* opinion, should you first see what your friends will say?"
- "Should you agree with someone because they're popular or you think they're smarter than you?"
- "Should you agree with someone because it's easier than thinking for yourself?"
- "Is it hard to be the only one who thinks a certain way?"
- "Should you disagree with someone because you feel like disagreeing?"

THE MAJORITY RULES

Needed: Chart paper to write down the question sets inserted within this conduit; optional downloaded picture of city streets in gridlock.

Democracy begins at the local level, and there is probably no better place for young minds to see how democracy works than in their own classrooms.

The path to having students make a group decision based on their opinions can sometimes be surprisingly smooth, with everyone immediately agreeing. At other times, compromising flies out the window, minds are indelibly made up, and an impasse dashes all hopes of arriving at a conclusive decision.

One primary solution to maneuvering around this obstacle is as old as our democracy: letting the majority rule. This form of decision making might already be used in your classroom, and it might not always be popular. Some children, especially younger ones, may think it's "unfair" if their choice loses by one vote.

Others may argue that the majority's opinion "is wrong," and some kids will immediately split the class into the "winning" side and the "losing" side.

This is inevitable, as many adults who have ever cast a vote in any election can attest to feeling the same way.

However, despite these viewpoints, using "the majority rules" in the classroom gets the students accustomed to employing a system that is embedded into our democracy and will be used in many other instances throughout their lives.

In addition, having the majority rule shows your students that they can arrive at a decision, even one that involves numerous viewpoints, as a democratic group that relies on its own opinions, not those of adults.

Explain to your students that for this activity, they'll be making decisions based on imaginary situations, raising their hands or flashing a thumbs up to signify which choice reflects their own opinions.

As always, try to ensure that all the children are voicing their opinions and that some students are not avoiding making a decision. Note when some kids are raising their hands only when their friends do and remind everyone that these decisions come from their own brains, not the brains of their friends.

As you present each question set, tally the students' opinions for each decision they have to make and conduct a run-off if the two top vote getters are tied. Forego asking the students to explain why they chose the options they did; later they will spend some time explaining what they think about using "the majority rules" as a solution for making group decisions.

These question sets are suggestions, but please insert alternatives that might be more reflective of your students' interests:

1. Where should we go on a trip?

    A. Beach
    B. Mountains
    C. Natural history museum
    D. Art museum
    E. Desert

2. What should we do during free time?

    A. Watch a movie
    B. Play board games
    C. Have quiet chat time
    D. Daydream
    E. Do puzzles

3. Which color should we paint the bookshelves?

    A. Red
    B. Purple
    C. Multicolored stripes

D. Yellow
   E. Green

4. What should we do in the talent show as a class?

   A. Sing
   B. Dance
   C. Recite a poem
   D. Tell jokes
   E. Act out a short play

When all the tallying is done, explain to the students that the choice with the most votes is the decision the group must go along with because that is what the majority, or most of the people, want.

Even if they don't like basing their decisions on what the majority dictates, do the students see any positive aspects to making decisions that way? If so, what are they? Do they think that using "the majority rules" can help them move forward in making group decisions and progress on whatever it is they're trying to accomplish? If so, how does it accomplish that?

If the students don't see any value in using "the majority rules," ask, "Do you have a different way of coming to a decision that could take the place of 'the majority rules?'" It would be interesting and noteworthy if someone does!

To finish this exercise, show the students a downloaded picture of gridlock in any major city and ask, "Is there a connection between what is happening here and what happens when people can't reach a decision?" "Can progress be made? Can anything move forward?"

OPEN MINDS

Kids can become incredibly proud of themselves when they feel they've convincingly expressed their opinions and presented good explanations for why they think what they think. But sometimes a monkey wrench gets thrown in.

All of a sudden, someone else comes along with astonishingly persuasive reasons why his or her opinion is the better idea. And while it might be hard to admit . . . it is a better way of thinking.

We encourage children to "speak their minds" and to give "their" opinions, not those of others. Yet we encourage them to have "open minds." So when a child thinks, "Gee, she *is* making more sense than I am," he might wonder, "Should I change my mind? Switch to her opinion? Stick with what I think because it's my opinion? If I change my mind, will it look like I was wrong?"

Present this story to spark your pupils into thinking about whether it's ever okay to change their minds or alter their opinions.

For last night's homework, Dakota had to express her opinions about Micah, a character in a novel she's reading. Today, she'll meet up with her language arts partner, Gabriella, to discuss those opinions and present them to the class.

Dakota spent a long time last night writing about Micah. She put a ton of energy into the assignment, and she can't wait to tell Gabriella that she's totally nailed Micah's character.

When the two girls meet, Dakota says, "I think Micah is arrogant and overconfident. He thinks he's better than everyone else. He's conceited and super proud."

Then Dakota gives a couple of examples of Micah's behavior to support her opinions.

Then it's Gabriella's turn: "Micah's not arrogant and proud. He's shy and confused, not snobby and conceited. And he's not overconfident. In fact, he doesn't have a lot of confidence."

Dakota thinks to herself, "Boy, did she get this wrong! There's no way Gabriella can support these opinions with good reasons. I know I'm right about Micah."

Before Dakota can say anything, Gabriella begins explaining why she thinks what she thinks. To Dakota's astonishment, Gabriella makes a lot of thoughtful, excellent points that support her opinions. She backs up everything she says with more evidence and facts than Dakota did. Dakota begins to doubt her own opinions. She really doesn't want to admit that though. She worked so hard on this assignment last night.

Yet all Dakota can think of is "Wow, Gabriella's right. I have been looking at Micah all wrong."

Give your students a minute to think about this story. Then ask, "What should Dakota do?"

    A. Dakota should change her opinion of Micah and agree with Gabriella.
    B. Dakota should stick with her opinion, even though she secretly agrees with Gabriella.

Open the discussion by asking the students to explain the reasons they chose *Option B, "Dakota should stick with her opinion, even though she secretly agrees with Gabriella."* While it may be difficult for Dakota to admit it, she knows Gabriella is right, and in the spirit of being open minded, Option B is not the best choice.

We want children to see that if they truly agree that someone else has "a better way to think"—no matter whether it's an idea, an opinion, or a solution—then they could and should change their thinking. It's the "bigger" person who says "You're right" and the "smarter" person who chooses an improvement when she or he sees it.

Do the students who chose Option B feel that Dakota shouldn't change her opinions of Micah because she spent so much time on the homework assignment? If so, you can ask, "Could Dakota change her mind if the assignment took her ten minutes to do?" "Should time matter?"

Would Dakota look foolish if she changed her mind? If some students think this, you can ask, "Is it foolish to stick with an idea you don't believe in when you know something better is out there?"

What reasons did the students give for making the wisest decision, *Option A, "Dakota should change her opinion of Micah and agree with Gabriella"*? After the students give their explanations, ask:

- "Should Dakota change her mind because it is the practical thing to do?" (Gabriella's explanations of Micah's character make more sense than Dakota's.)
- "Do you think that Dakota and Gabriella will get a better grade if Dakota agrees with Gabriella?"
- "Are you a better person if you admit that you're changing your mind because someone else's idea or opinion makes more sense to you?"

A key question to ask your students is "Are there times when you shouldn't change your mind or opinion?" If you've already presented the "Back it Up" prompt in this section, your students may have addressed this, but some reinforcement could be helpful.

If some students believe there are certain instances when a person shouldn't change his or her mind, what are they? Is bending to peer pressure one instance? Can your students articulate the differences between changing their minds for a more sensible and valuable reason versus going along with someone just because that person is a friend or it's the easiest route to take?

FILL IN THE BLANKS

Needed: Chart for writing down the example sentences; one copy for each student of the fill-in-the-blank sentence that appears at the end of the conduit.

Opinions are based on what people think. That is true, but the reasons given to defend those opinions are just as important as the opinions themselves.

Tell your students that this is a fill-in-the-blank exercise *and* a game. Explain to them that they'll be expressing their opinions about something and explaining their reasons for those opinions to their partners. The game rests on the clues (reasons) the partners give each other.

There are a few steps to this prompt:

1. Distribute the fill-in-the-blank sentence at the end of the prompt to each student. To illustrate how the students should fill in the blanks, put this example on the chart or create your own: "In my opinion, I think *the roller coaster* (student's choice) is the best *amusement park ride* (category) because *it's exciting to be on when it goes fast and swoops up and down while it's on the track* (reasons)."

2. Read the sentence to your students and explain to them that the first blank is for *anything they think is the best* in any category; the second blank is for that *category* (feel free to set your own category parameters [for example, maybe no video games]), and the third blank is for *the reasons that will support their opinions*.

3. Emphasize that the reasons the students give for their opinions should be supported with as many facts and as much evidence as possible. That information will act as clues to help their partners figure out what they're talking about.

Explain to the students, "When you read your sentence to your teammate, you'll be *leaving out the words to the first two blanks*. The only blank you'll fill in as you're reading is the one that follows 'because.' Your partner will have to figure out your *best thing and its category* based only on your reasons."

4. Let the students read along as you model what they should do. "I'm going to read the sentence about roller coasters again, but I'm going to read it the way I would to my partner to make him or her figure out what I'm talking about: "In my opinion, I think *blank* is the best *blank* because *it's exciting to be on when it goes fast and swoops up and down while it's on the track.*"

(To make it simpler for younger students, you could write a few different categories—best food, book, movie, etc.—into the second fill in the blank before you distribute the sentences. Just make sure that when you pair up the partners, they don't have the same category. With the category already written in, the students will only have to supply responses for the first and last blanks; their partners will only have to determine what the best thing is.)

5. Give the students several minutes to work on their sentences. Then pair them up with a partner (if there's an odd number, one group can be a trio) and let them read their sentences to each other.

If, as the game progresses, some students are having trouble determining their partner's best thing and category, instruct their classmates to fill in the second category blank for them. If they still don't know what the best thing is, have the students add different reasons that will help back up their opinions.

When all the sharing is completed, ask the students:

- "Do you think your reasons were helpful to your partner? Why/why not?"
- "Did your reasons support your opinion? Why/why not?"
- "Can reasons be helpful to back up your opinions? Why/why not?"

You can have different versions of this exercise—for example, the students could choose the "worst" thing in a category.

In my opinion, I think _____

is the best _____

because _____.

SHOULD I OR SHOULDN'T I?

There are times when even the most outspoken, opinionated children can be taken aback when an awkward situation makes them wonder if voicing their opinions is worth a potential risk. The question can quickly morph from "What is your opinion?" to "Should I give you my opinion?"

This territory is not new to any adult who has struggled with whether or not to keep a certain opinion to oneself. If adults grapple with questions like these, how must children feel in similar situations?

For this conduit, there are some option answers to get the discussion underway. However, as with the prompt "Honest Opinion?" in this section, the scenario falls into that gray area in which the right decision may be different for different people. With this in mind, the query posed at the end of this scenario is simply "What would you feel the most comfortable doing?"

Depending on your students' personalities and their own comfort levels, there may be a real difference of "opinion" on their reactions to this situation.

You've joined a new book club. Everyone is giving their opinions on which book the club should read next. You have a different book you'd like to suggest, but you feel funny about speaking up because you're new to the group, and you're the youngest person there.

"What would you feel the most comfortable doing?"

A. Not saying anything because you're new and the youngest person.
B. Giving your opinion because, after all, you're still a club member.
C. Agree to read the book most members want to read next even though you don't want to read it.

When the students defend their choices, ask them, "Why did this option make you feel more comfortable than the others?"

Have your students think a little deeper by asking those who chose *Option A, "Not saying anything because you're new and the youngest person,"* this question: "Why is it better to keep silent if you're new or the youngest person?" "How long should you wait before you can express your opinion? Is the second meeting okay?"

For those pupils who choose *Option B, "Giving your opinion because, after all, you're still a club member,"* you can ask, "Why doesn't it matter if you're new and the youngest?"

And for those students who chose *Option C, "Agreeing to read the book most members want to read next even though you don't want to read it,"* you can ask, "Could choosing this option make it easier to become friends with some of the members because you agreed with them?"

At the end of the discussion, you can ask the class, "Can anyone tell us about a similar situation that you were in and what you said?" Feel free to describe your own experience.

HONEST OPINION?

As with the conduit "Should I or Shouldn't I?" in this section, the following prompt falls into that nebulous category of decision making in which there aren't any precise right or wrong responses.

This type of situation can be puzzling to children who don't want to "lie" but may not be prepared to tell someone what they really think because they don't want to hurt their feelings.

Your friend gets a new haircut. You don't think it suits him. You hope he doesn't ask you if you like it. So far, so good. You've been able to distract him by talking about your favorite TV show. Then your heart sinks when he says, "Hey, didn't you notice my new haircut? Isn't it awesome?"

"Should you tell your friend your honest opinion?"

A. Yes, give him your honest opinion because that's what he wants.
B. No, don't tell him what you're thinking because it will hurt his feelings.
C. Find one good thing about the haircut and tell him about it.
D. Pretend you didn't hear the question.

Some students may elect to go the whole honesty route with *Option A, "Yes, give him your honest opinion because that's what he wants."* Do the students who chose this option believe that honesty is an important characteristic in a friend? If so, you can ask them, "Is it the responsibility of a good friend to give an honest opinion, no matter the consequences?"

You can also ask, "Is it more important to give an honest opinion than worrying about hurting your friend's feelings?" "If you speak honestly now, do you think your friend will ask for your honest opinion ever again?"

Do the students who chose *Option B, "No, don't tell him what you're thinking because it will hurt his feelings,"* think that telling a "fib" is okay because it can avoid making someone feel bad?

Within minutes, this conversation could turn into a thought-provoking dialogue about the difference between a fib and a lie and whether or not it's ever okay to tell either one. Let your students take this interesting path to wherever it leads.

Option C, "Find one good thing about the haircut and tell him about it," may be a way to soften the truth and still not "fib." Why did the students choose this option? Do they view it as a kind of "compromise" between Option A and B?

Option D, "Pretend you didn't hear the question," is unfortunately something that even adults would admit to doing. While there isn't a wrong or right choice for this scenario, Option D is doable, but it is the least favorable option.

It's possible that students who chose this decision felt it would give them time to think of a better answer. It might get them off the hook for a few seconds, but the friend may ask again. Maybe they are counting on continually distracting the friend so he forgets about his haircut. It may not come up again immediately, but there is no guarantee it won't come up another day.

Chapter Five

Streamlining

Two of the most difficult things for many children to accomplish are narrowing down their choices when they must make decisions and coping with organizational skills.

When some children add into this already complex mix their tendency to give every decision, choice, and problem the same importance, the result can be a lot of anxiety and frustration, and it can be counterproductive to decision making.

Teaching kids to ask themselves questions and to take the time to think about what's really important to them and how to eliminate certain choices can help them navigate a wide open field of decisions, as well as help them organize their thoughts . . . and their cubbies.

Helping children learn how to categorize, eliminate, qualify, prioritize, and distinguish between what's wanted and what's not wanted can assist them in their organizational skills and when they have to narrow down their choices.

These tactics can let them see that not everything has to have the same amount of importance or weight. Moreover, when they successfully use these strategies, some of that anxiety can be eased and result in a big sigh of relief.

STUFF

A cluttered, disheveled desk was the perfect work place for Albert Einstein, but that doesn't mean being disorganized is ideal for everyone . . . or for an entire classroom of children.

The habits and natures of some kids equip them to casually sail through disarray, coping perfectly well even if that disarray causes them some occasional consternation.

For other kids, especially those needing guidance with their own organizational skills, a topsy-turvy environment can derail them from going about their daily routines in a calm, stress-free way.

Read these two poems first, and then pose the various questions. The purpose of this prompt is to help children think about whether or not they're making the best choices for themselves about being organized or disorganized and how those choices impact themselves and maybe others.

As their teacher, you may gain some insight into why your students make certain decisions about their personal space.

Stuff: Version One

I'm losing my mind
Because I can't find
Anything I need at all
No shoes, no shirt, no soccer ball.

Well, at least I found a hat for my head,
But how did it ever get in the cat's bed?
It always makes me worry, worry, worry
When I've got to hurry, hurry, hurry
Out the front door
When I still have to look some more . . .
What's this? A soggy sandwich of PB and J?
Oh no! Didn't I finish that last Wednesday?

There's so much junk in this tangle of clutter,
I can't believe what I'm about to mutter:
"I've had enough, enough, enough!
"It's really time to clean out this stuff!"

Stuff: Version Two

I haven't lost my mind,
I just can't find
Anything at all,
No shoes, no shirt, no soccer ball.

Well, at least I found a hat for my head,
Isn't this funny? It was in the cat's bed!
I never ever worry, worry, worry
When I have to hurry, hurry, hurry
Out the front door
Yeah, I know I have to look some more . . .
Hah! Here's that soggy sandwich of PB and J
Maybe I'll throw it away another day!

There's so much terrific junk in all this clutter,
I don't know why it makes my mom shudder.

I'll never have enough, enough, enough
Of all this gorgeous, messy stuff!

When you're done reading, let the students describe what happens in each poem, contrasting the differences between the narrators' reactions in both versions. Then ask, "Should both of the narrators make a decision to become more organized? Why/why not?"

The students may explain that since narrator #1 has had it with not being able to find necessary stuff, that she or he should change his or her ways. On the other hand, the students may think that a change isn't needed for narrator #2 because she or he isn't bothered by his or her mess. In reference to narrator #2, however, you could ask, "Do you think she or he should make a choice to be neater if all that clutter bothers other family members?"

Have the kids dig a little deeper into their own styles: "Think about how you do things. Do you do things in an organized way, or a disorganized way—for example, when you do your work, is everything neat or disorganized?"

After they reflect for a minute or so, ask for a thumbs up or thumbs down: "Which way do you act most of the time?"

A. Disorganized
B. Organized

After the votes are in, tell the students: "Think about whether or not the way you act most times is the best way for you. For example, does being disorganized ever cause you problems? Does being organized ever cause problems? Does the way you act make you feel comfortable or uncomfortable?"

Then ask the students who gave a thumbs up for *Option A, "Disorganized"*:

- "What do you like about being disorganized?"
- "Are there disadvantages to being disorganized?"
- "Are you happy being disorganized or would you like to be a little organized? Why/why not?"
- "If you'd like to be more organized, how could you start doing that?"
- "Could your life could be easier if you were less disorganized? If so, how? If not, why not?"

Ask similar questions of the students who chose *Option B, "Organized"*:

- "What do you like about being organized?"
- "Are there disadvantages to being organized?"
- "Are you happy being organized or would you like to be a little disorganized? Why/why not?"

- "Could your life be easier if you were less organized? If so, how? If not, why not?"

Extend the conversation by asking, "Could your being disorganized or organized affect others? If so, how? If not, why not?"

WRITE ABOUT "ANYTHING"

Explain to your students that they have an assignment to write an essay about anything they want. Many students become uncomfortable or unnerved when given such a wide berth without any specifics. Ask your students, "Which option is the best starting point to help you decide what to write about?"

   A. Think of topics you like or that interest you.
   B. Ask your friends what they are doing and use one of their topics.
   C. Ask an adult to choose the topic for you.

Option A, "Think of topics you like or that interest you," makes the most sense and would be the most helpful. After your students explain their reasons for choosing this option, if someone doesn't already say this, ask them, "Does time pass more quickly when you're doing something you like to do or when you're bored? Do you have a better time if you're interested in something or if you 'have to do' something?"

For most people, time does pass faster when they like what they're doing, and people often do their best work when they like something or it interests them. It will be easier for students to write about something they can relate to or feel ownership in rather than write about a mandated subject. There will be many times when specific assignments will be handed out. Suggest to your students that an assignment like this one is a gift because they get to choose. (And they get to practice decision making!)

Thinning the field of essay topics to a single category (those that are liked or are of interest) shows your students one simple way to make an overwhelming decision more manageable.

Option B, "Ask your friends what they are doing and use one of their topics," is a no-no. Do the students who liked this option see that using a friend's topic would be taking his or her idea? You can ask, "Will your friend like that you took his or her idea?" Every educator has seen how a classroom discussion can teeter on the brink of disruption when someone yells out, "Hey, that was *my* idea!"

You can also ask, "What will the teacher say when he or she sees two ideas that are exactly the same?"

Furthermore, you can explain to your students that their friend's idea may not truly reflect their own interests. This also reinforces that Option A is the best choice because it would give them a chance to write an essay that follows their own interests.

Option C, "Ask an adult to choose the topic for you," is, like Option B, a no-no because it reflects passing off making a decision to someone else and results in the students not doing their own thinking, which is part of the assignment.

TOO MANY LIBRARY BOOKS!

Begin this exercise by briefly reinforcing the benefits of a visit to the school library. Then read this brief excerpt:

Imagine you're in the library. You're ready to check out a ton of books. But you realize you can't carry all of them. What's the least sensible decision you could make about all those books?

- A. Ask yourself some questions about each book, such as, "Have I waited a long time for this book? Do I need it for a project?" Choose the books you want or need the most and return the rest to the shelves.
- B. Ask a friend for help carrying the books.
- C. Tell the librarian you'll make two trips for the books.
- D. Slide out some books from the stack—it doesn't matter which ones—and return them to the shelves.

Option D, "Slide out some books from the stack—it doesn't matter which ones—and return them to the shelves," may be an appealing choice to many students because it seems like the "easiest" decision, but it is the *least sensible* one.

Do the students defend this as the *least sensible* option because they see that it could result in leaving the books they wanted or needed the most behind? Do some students explain that this choice isn't a real decision—it's letting *chance* make the decision for them?

When the students discuss their choices, note that some of them may have assumed that they were to choose the *most sensible* option. Take a moment to remind them that listening and reading carefully are important skills to use at all times.

Let's take a look at *Option A, "Ask yourself some questions about each book, such as, 'Have I waited a long time for this book? Do I need it for a project?' Choose the books you want or need the most and return the rest to the shelves."* Did anyone classify this as the least sensible decision? If so, how do they defend their reasoning?

Some students might view this as the least sensible option because they think it would take too long to assess the books. You can ask them, "What would be better in the long run: to take some time now to go through the books or go home without the books you want?"

Ask anyone who chose *Option B, "Ask a friend for help carrying the books,"* or *Option C, "Tell the librarian you'll make two trips for the books,"* as the least sensible decisions to explain their reasoning behind these choices. Someone might say, "I don't want to ask a friend" or "I don't want to make two trips." Again, ask them what would be preferable: "Which would be better: going home without the books you want or asking a friend or making two trips to the library?"

Once the students discuss their least sensible options, expand the discussion about why Options A, B, and C are good choices.

Option A urges kids to ask themselves certain questions to help them make a choice. When students ask questions of themselves, that can be a big step forward toward being active and judicious decision makers. See if the class can think of any other questions that could help decide which books to check out. Maybe "Have I already read this book? Do I have this book at home?"

By asking specific questions, the students can weed something out or leave something in.

The thought process used to narrow down the library books is similar to the steps kids can use when crafting other decisions, such as which games to play, what to eat for lunch, when to start doing homework, or the myriad other decisions they make on a daily basis.

The two other options, *Option B, "Ask a friend for help carrying the books,"* and *Option C, "Tell the librarian you'll make two trips for the books,"* allow the bookworms to sidestep making specific reading decisions, but they are still acceptable choices.

Option B gives you a chance to have your students think about the different kinds of help a friend can give. You can ask, "Is there a difference between asking a friend to help carry your library books and asking them to do your homework?" "If so, what is it; if not, why not?"

You can extend the thinking for this conduit by posing one more question: "Let's say that you made two trips to the library or asked a friend to help carry your library books. How will you get all of those books home?"

RECIPE FOR FRIENDSHIP

Needed: Two-column chart labeled "Pat's Ingredients"; "Friendship Ingredients."

Friendships are incredibly emotional relationships, and sometimes it's difficult for kids, with their open hearts, to see that someone they think is a friend is not really a friend at all.

For this two-part conduit, your students will describe their own "friendship ingredients"—those qualities they think make up a good friend. Then they will see whether those characteristics match up with the traits of a fictitious friend in the story you'll present.

Older students might view this activity as similar to crafting an outline for a book report or an essay. By having the students describe their self-authored ingredients for a good pal, they're making a blueprint for what they see as important traits in a friend. They are winnowing the field of all the possible personality characteristics to those qualities they see as essential in a friend. They are, in essence, bringing some practicality into an emotional decision.

To model what your students will do, draw a large outline of a child's face on a piece of paper. Inside the drawing, write any word you think is an indispensable attribute to have in a wonderful friend.

Explain to your students that you are making a "good friend" and you want them to create their own good friends. Ask them to draw an outline of a child's face and then fill it with "ingredients" that a good friend would possess. Depending on your grade level, you may want to set a minimum/maximum number of ingredients or keep it open ended.

To make the ensuing friendship discussion easier, let's keep this illustrated friend anonymous and tell the students not to name their friend. This will help avoid disruptive conversations over "who drew who."

Once the children have finished their sketches, fill in the column on the chart labeled *"Friendship Ingredients"* with the qualities the kids think are essential in a good friend. Some ingredients may overlap—for example, many kids might say "kindness"—but you should still wind up with a decent cross-section of characteristics.

Once this is done, ask your students to put aside their sketches while you read this story about Pat, whose flaws mimic many of the complaints kids have about their "friends."

You are friends with Pat, but Pat often does things you don't like. Sometimes Pat lies to you. A lot of times, Pat won't play with you, even though you agreed to play together on a certain day. Sometimes Pat makes fun of you. Pat often ignores you while playing with other kids. When you do play with Pat, you don't have fun.

After the story is presented, pose this question: "Should you keep Pat as a friend?"

A. Yes, I should keep Pat as a friend.
B. I am not sure if Pat should be my friend.
C. No, I should not keep Pat as my friend.

Before you ask the kids about their responses, ask them to tell you what Pat's qualities are and write them down in the *"Pat's Ingredients"* column.

Begin the discussion by asking if anyone chose *Option A, "Yes, I should keep Pat as a friend,"* or Option B, *"I am not sure if Pat should be my friend."* How do these students defend their reasons for keeping Pat as a friend or being unsure about Pat?

Ask them to look at their own friendship ingredients and/or those on the chart that were chosen from all the character traits a person could have. Does Pat possess any of these qualities? If the answer is "No," should Pat still be their friend? If they answer "Yes," ask them to point out the parts of the story that show that Pat has those qualities.

Ask the students who are undecided about Pat's friendship why they can't make up their minds. There are times all of us are unsure about something. We might need more time to think or more facts or proof before we can make an informed decision. However, it is worthwhile to note if certain students continually say "I'm not sure" so they can avoid making a decision. Remind your students that these exercises are to help them practice thinking and making choices.

Sometimes kids have difficulty equating actions—their own or others—with what's on their minds. For instance, kids who can't make up their minds about Pat or think Pat should remain their friend may have had "being nice" as one of their friendship ingredients.

Yet they might think that "being mean" is one of Pat's qualities. To help them think further, ask, "Is being mean the opposite of being nice?" "Is lying or making fun of you being mean or not being nice?"

You can have the students further evaluate Pat's traits by asking, "What would a friend have to do to make you stop being their friend?" "Do any of Pat's actions fall into this category?"

Can your students draw parallels or distinctions between what they value in a good friend and someone's behavior?

Ask the students who chose *Option C, "No, I should not keep Pat as my friend,"* which would be the healthiest choice, to defend their reasons. Do they point out that Pat does not have the characteristics a friend should have? Do they see the parallel between Pat's actions and what they value in a friend?

If you want to extend this prompt further, use a math analogy. Write down two easy questions like "5 + 5 = ?" and "4 + 1 = ?" on a chart or board. Then write down the two correct answers along with some wrong answers. Ask your students which choices are correct. They'll yell out "10" and "5" with extreme confidence, as well as some doubt as to why you're asking such simple questions.

You can then ask, "Are '10 and 5' the choices that matched up to the right answers?" They will say "Yes."

You can then explain that choosing the right math answers is like choosing a friend with the right friendship ingredients: "When you choose a good friend, does it make sense to choose someone whose qualities don't match up to your own right ingredients?"

MIXED UP

As discussed earlier in this section, some children are perfectly content to be disorganized within their own personal space. It is the daunting challenge of educators to enlighten them so they recognize that being organized is a key element that can help certain tasks consume less time, run smoother, and ward off future problems.

Being organized requires asking astute questions and making thoughtful decisions. This conduit will give your students a chance to practice their organizational skills by imagining that they are going to participate in a school-wide project:

To raise money for hurricane victims, our grade is going to sell seeds that people can use to grow plants, trees, fruits, vegetables, and flowers. We already have many boxes filled with thousands of packets of seeds, but the packets are all mixed up.

Students and adults will sell the seeds in the school parking lot next Saturday to anyone who would like to buy them. It will be exciting to help with this project, but first we have to figure out how to organize all those seeds! We want to make it easy so that when a customer says "I'd like some watermelon seeds," we can do that quickly and easily.

Before you ask the students for their specific organizing ideas, ask them, "Would we really need to organize the seeds? Couldn't we just put the boxes out on the tables and let the customers look for what they want?"

    A. Yes, I think we should organize the seeds.
    B. No, I don't think we should organize the seeds.

The students who chose *Option A, "Yes, I think we should organize the seeds,"* are correct in thinking that a task of this magnitude needs some organization to avoid confusion for everyone. After the students defend their reasons, if they haven't already addressed these topics, you can ask:

- "Is being organized the most efficient way to sell the seeds? Why/why not?"
- "Will organizing the seeds make it easier to find what the customers need? If so, how?"
- "Could being organized possibly help the students sell more seeds? If so, how?"

How do the students defend their choice of *Option B, "No, I don't think we should organize the seeds"*? If they don't believe that organizing is necessary, ask, "If you don't organize the seeds, how would you sell them?"

If they think having the customers browse through the boxes or spreading the seed packets on the tables are good alternatives, ask, "How will those ideas make selling the seeds less hectic and more efficient than if you organized them?"

When the students describe their other "nonorganized" alternatives, listen carefully. Their ideas may actually rest on some sort of organization without them realizing it.

By the end of the discussion the students will hopefully see that the most efficient way to sell the seeds is to organize them. You can then ask, "What's the best way to organize the seeds? Remember, there are five types: plants, trees, fruits, vegetables, and flowers."

Give the students a chance to brainstorm—toss out various ideas and then narrow them down to the most sensible and practical ones. Look for a semblance of logic when the students offer their suggestions. If some kids say, "Let's arrange everything by color!" see if, upon further reflection, they can articulate why this wouldn't be a practical idea.

The two most logical ways to organize the seeds would be to divide them into categories (flowers, plants, etc.) and then arrange them alphabetically within those categories. (Category: Flowers; then A for asters, etc.) Your students may arrive at this solution, but they may also come up with something else that's creative and sensible!

If the students agree to organize the seeds by category, you can further ask, "Is there a way to narrow down the categories?" Older students might know that tree seeds can be further divided into the coniferous and deciduous varieties, and fruits can be separated into those that have pits or stones and those that carry seeds.

ZEROING IN

Needed: One three-column chart labeled "Where"; "Why It's a Problem"; "Solution."

A lot of time and effort goes into transforming the four walls of a classroom into a second home that is a nurturing and safe environment for every student.

While much of this emotional comfort comes from an intangible quality, some of it can also emanate from the more practical and physical aspects of the classroom. A room layout or design that worked well one year may not fit with a different group of students the following year. This year's students may keep their cubbies impeccably neat, but next year's class may find that a daily challenge.

Tell your students you need their help for a real-life project that will find the best way for everyone in the classroom to live more comfortably together.

I've been wondering if any of you have some ideas of how we could change or fix certain things in our classroom to make it easier for all of us to move around, to be more comfortable, or to just make it a better place for us to live.

You might already have something in mind, but let's also take a couple of minutes now to look around the room. Take your time and be observant. Do you see something that's a problem area or something that could be improved? If you want to get out of your seats and walk around, you may do so quietly.

When the students offer their ideas, make sure they describe *"Where"* the problem is, *"Why It's a Problem,"* and the *"Solution"* or how it can be fixed.

For example, "We need to do *something about the cubbies ("Where") because stuff is always falling on the floor and people can trip on it ("Why It's a Problem"). Maybe we can have a chart to remind us to clean them out every Wednesday ("Solution")* so they won't be as jam-packed."

As the students make their suggestions, write them down on the labeled, three-column chart. If five kids say the closet is always a mess, only list it once in the *"Where"* and *"Why It's a Problem"* categories, but include every *"Solution"* that is offered.

Asking the students "Which *problem* should you fix first and why?" could result in a lot of kids saying, "The cubbies because they're messy" and an equal number of kids declaring, "The closet because that's messy."

Try asking a different initial question, one that focuses on the *kind* of problem to attack first. Initially, approaching the situation this way may seem like a lot to go through just to figure out how to clean up a room. However, this can be another way for your students to view a cluster of problems and could help them establish clearer reasons why something should be a priority and why something else should be last on the list.

Please feel free to add or substitute options that might be more reflective of the suggestions your students made for your classroom.

"Which *kind* of problem is the most important and should be fixed first?"

A. The kind of problem that bothers the most people
B. The kind of problem that would be the hardest to fix
C. The kind of problem that would be the easiest to fix

Once the students have determined the kind of problem they want to tackle first, have them decide which problems on the chart fall into that category. For instance, if the students agree they should start with the problem that bothers the most people (Option A), ask them to vote for the *specific* problem on the chart that bothers them the most.

The cubbies and the closet might be messy, but the kids may realize that one of them is more bothersome and needs more immediate attention than the other. Thinking of the problem area in this way can help qualify their thinking.

Once the voting is completed, the students will have their own game plan and an ordered list of problems and remedies they can undertake to make their classroom a better place to live. They will have done this in a systematic, streamlined, and organized manner by looking at the entire classroom and bringing the focus to a few problematic areas.

To end the discussion, ask your students, "Did you make any progress from when you first looked around the room to where you are now?"

PICK A NUMBER, ANY NUMBER!

Children often complain that they don't get a choice about making some decisions they feel are theirs to make. Ironically, when they must make certain decisions, a common objection can be that there are "too many things to think about."

Use this prompt to spur your students into thinking logically while having them see that the process of elimination can be their friend when they make choices. They'll also see that setting parameters is another technique that can help them make skillful decisions.

Announce to the class, "I am thinking of a number. What is it?"

The kids will complain that they can't possibly figure out the number or they'll shout out any numbers that pop into their heads. If, by some weird coincidence, someone does guess your number, explain that this is a rarity and try again. It would be highly unlikely it would happen twice.

After you tell the pupils that none of their guesses are correct, ask, "Why can't you figure out what number I'm thinking of?"

Although the responses will vary, the gist of their answers will be that the choices are infinite. Congratulate your students on their astute thinking and begin setting parameters around the number in your head.

Here's an example of how it could go: Let's say your number is eighteen. After the kids throw out their initial random guesses, you can say, "Okay, I'll make it easy. It's less than ten thousand." This will elicit more complaints and random guesses. Depending on how much time you have, you can narrow the window quickly or slowly. As you run through various layers of numbers that span large ranges, the kids will be randomly guessing.

Eventually, however, you'll arrive at a point like this: "The number is between ten and twenty." Then be more specific: "One digit is odd; one digit is even." Lastly: "The sum of its digits is nine."

You can use any qualifiers you want and make the game last as long or as short as you want. When the number is ultimately determined, ask the class, "Why were you finally able to discover the number I had in my head?"

Do the students think that logic and facts helped them figure it out? Did your descriptions of the number—getting more and more specific, a narrower and narrower window—help them decide what it was? If so, why was that helpful? Could this kind of thinking help them make decisions in their own lives? If so, how? If not, why not?

You can explain to the class that while they may think of this as a guessing game, they eventually figured out the number based on facts, not guesses or assumptions.

If you have time, you can extend this idea of setting parameters with a game of "I Spy." Do the students see any parallels between discovering what the "Spy" sees and figuring out the mystery number that was in your head?

Chapter Six

Side by Side

Lin-Manuel Miranda, creator and star of the Broadway musical "Hamilton," says that it's "proven" that "working with other people just makes you smarter."

Increased brain power alone, then, would be a good enough reason to teach children how to work together. But in addition to Miranda's claim, collaboration also teaches kids to respect the viewpoints of others, to join forces for a common goal, to speak their minds, and to take pride in accomplishing something collectively.

And while it is inevitable that some children don't like working in groups, it would be a disservice not to give them opportunities to engage in collaboration. This is a lifelong skill that is needed in all grades, in the workforce, and generally in life.

Collaboration takes practice, and even in the most collegial of classrooms, some common pitfalls can plague any group dynamic. It's often easier to have certain guidelines in place that can help sidestep some of these problems before they become major obstacles. Here are some suggestions:

- Have a set routine for how the students will make their presentations. They can elect one student to represent the group, have each student speak, or have one student start the presentation and others can chime in.
- If one student will represent (or lead) the group, have the kids choose that student by asking each other, "Does anyone *want* to be the group representative?" "Was anyone a rep lately?" "Should we use majority rules and vote for a representative?" There is always the tried and true: "One potato, two potato . . ." or "Rock, paper, scissors . . ." to choose.

- Let the students know in advance how much time they will have for their collaborative work. Give them a heads up half way through, then another a few minutes before the time is up.
- Some children will consistently "hog" the discussion time, leaving others with little or no time to have their say. Remind the kids that everyone should get a chance to contribute. The students can try to remedy this on their own, but that can sometimes lead to more turmoil. This is something you can monitor as you observe the kids, and you can step in to arbitrate as frustration creeps in. Conversely, you can monitor if some kids are holding back and not contributing.

If your students continually have difficulties working together in either large or small groups, let them practice making choices together by asking them to collaborate on one simple question at a time instead of on a grand project or assignment.

For example, you can ask, "Where should we hang the class rules?" It may not seem like a big deal to an adult, but when kids make even tiny decisions like these in their own classrooms, it gives them a sense of ownership and pride and a chance to work at teamwork.

Anytime your students work together, ask them to rate their collaborative skills: Did they work well together? Why/why not? What should be done next time? What could be done better next time? What did they succeed at? What was the most troublesome part?

MEET THE INVENTORS

Needed: Crayons, colored pencils, markers.

For this prompt, each group of students (preferably three, but four could work) chooses something to invent: new kind of shoe, new time-saving device, new game (not a video one), new amusement park ride, new kind of car, or a new kind of flying machine. (Please feel free to add your own inventions—maybe something essential for your classroom!)

Observe how the students make their collective decisions. Do they easily choose their inventions? Do they keep changing their minds and delay making a decision? Do they immediately freeze up? Is saying "No" to every idea someone's favorite word? Can the students come to a consensus as a group?

Invariably there will be some dissension and arguments, but somewhere along the line, agreement usually comes along. If choosing becomes impossible, with some students freezing up, others drifting from idea to idea, or some simply saying "No," try asking pertinent questions that might nudge the students into narrowing down their decisions: "Do you have a favorite food? Do you wish you had more time in the day?"

When you ask questions like these, you are modeling some of the same questions your students could be asking themselves.

The students can always use "the majority rules" to come to an agreement. If there's a tie, ask the kids how they should resolve it. Let your students see that there are often many ways to solve a problem—they just have to think it through.

Supply your students with the paper, crayons, pencils, markers, and so on that they will need to draw their inventions and write about them.

Once the invention is chosen, tell your students to begin their thinking process by brainstorming—throwing out all kinds of ideas, even nutty ones. (See "Why Brainstorming?" on page 64)

While the inventors are having fun, this project can also be entertaining and instructional for the educators who observe them. An open-ended project can be a chance to see how the students blend their creative and logical thought processes in real time.

When the students explain their inventions to the class, ask some questions about how practical or logical the inventions are. "Does the invention make sense? What will make it work? How will it work? What is it made of?"

If the students can only claim that their new time-saving device "will save time," ask, "How it will do that?" If they've invented a new car but don't know what will make it run, they need to do more thinking.

Have the students explain their thought processes by asking:

- "Did you and your partners ask yourselves certain questions that helped you come up with your invention? If, yes, what were they?"
- "Were some ideas creative but not practical?"
- "Which decision was the most important one you and your partners made to create this invention?"

Allow the class to ask questions of the inventors too. You can do this as the students explain each invention or wait until all the explanations are completed. What kinds of questions are the students asking each other? Are they pointing out potential flaws in the practicality of the inventions and offering suggestions? Praising the ingenuity of the inventions?

This would be a good time to talk to the class about the merits of "constructive criticism."

GORILLA OR ELEPHANT?

Needed: Optional crayons, colored pencils, and markers.

Sometimes something a little silly can go a long way in teaching certain concepts. It might be a quirky game that reinforces math skills, a story that entices kids to read (was anyone sillier than Dr. Seuss?), or a ridiculous question that sparks your students into thinking something through and making prudent choices.

Divide your class into groups of three to five children. Tell the students there's a very important question they need to answer: "Would you rather give a gorilla a bath or take an elephant for a walk?" Remind the groups that they somehow must agree on which task to tackle.

Hopefully, this dilemma will be amusing but will nonetheless lead to thought-provoking, productive discussions about making choices. If you have enough time, in addition to conducting the discussion, you can have your students draw sketches that depict the tasks they chose.

While the conduit's premise is fantasy, let your students realistically argue with each other about why one animal should be chosen over the other. The students must give their peers concrete reasons and examples for why they think what they do.

When the students state their choices to the class, ensure that they go beyond "We like elephants, so we're walking the elephant." Instead, for example, ask questions that will prod them to think about why they chose their animal: "Which characteristic do you like about an elephant?" "Would this characteristic make walking an elephant an easier task than bathing a gorilla?" "Why/why not?" You can also ask:

- "Is bathing a gorilla more fun than walking an elephant (or vice-versa)? Why/why not?"
- "Is walking an elephant safer than giving a gorilla a bath? Why/why not?"
- "Will one task be more tiring than the other? If yes, how so?"
- "What would you use as a leash for an elephant?"
- "How much water do you need to give a gorilla a bath?"

When the groups have given their explanations and backed up their reasons, ask the students if thinking logically or sensibly helped them make their preposterous choices. If so, ask further: "If sensible and logical thinking can help with a choice like this, do you think that taking the time to think this way might help you make more important choices?"

If you want to challenge the class a little more, ask, "Did you think choosing between walking an elephant and bathing a gorilla was silly? Would it be silly if you worked in a zoo?"

Hmmm . . .

JUGGLING ACT

Sometimes the most obvious solutions are the ones that are ignored. Read this passage to your students and see if they can come up with an alternative to simply having more arms!

Your family has many things it would like to donate to a shelter for other families. You need to carry some items a few blocks from where your car is parked to where the shelter is located. You are carrying a ton of stuff, and things keep falling down onto the sidewalk. You move the things around and juggle them as best as you can, but everything keeps falling. You need more arms!

Here is what you are carrying:

- *one little, pink rubber ball*
- *an empty backpack*
- *two boys' T-shirts*
- *one baby's dress*
- *two small children's picture books*
- *lunch box*
- *checkers board and checkers*
- *baseball cap*
- *brand new box of crayons*
- *a baby doll*

Is there a better, more practical way to carry all of the stuff?

Divide the kids into small groups and give them a chance to brainstorm and toss their ideas around. When they share their solutions with the group, see if they combined creativity with practicality. Kids are often more creative and ingenious than adults when it comes to questions like these. Keep an eye out for creativity, but also ensure that the suggested solutions are practical and workable.

When they describe their solutions, ask the students what makes their solutions more sensible than the one presented in the prompt? If they say, "Well, stuff won't fall this way," ask, "Why won't it fall?" Sometimes kids assume we know how they're thinking and don't feel they have to sufficiently explain their answers. But asking questions, even when the answers seem obvious, helps kids practice qualifying their answers and articulating their reasons.

Does anyone mention that some of the things could be packed into the backpack and lunchbox? If so, have them be specific—which items would go where? What would still have to be carried? Can a checkers board fit into a backpack? Does anyone suggest wearing the baseball cap as a way to transport it instead of carrying it?

Does anyone advocate asking someone for help? Making two trips?

When all the sharing is done, you can ask, "Which way is better? To keep juggling the stuff around and letting it fall or taking the time to figure out a better way to carry everything?"

SIX WORDS

Whether a decision needs to be made quickly or can marinate in the luxury of time, asking the right questions can be the best starting point to making a sound choice.

Kids can often feel at sea, not knowing how to start making a decision or where to begin sorting through a tangle of choices. Inspiring them to ask themselves questions about those decisions can be the engine that generates a solid, constructive decision instead of an ineffective or unproductive one.

This collaborative thinking exercise is twofold: first, to make a decision about what kind of worthy cause your students want to raise money for; and second, how to raise that money. If you want to transform this exercise into a real-life classroom situation, giving the students the opportunity to make these choices will give them a stronger sense of pride and ownership in this project, rather than simply having adults dictate the decision.

Explain to the students that they will be performing a fundraiser to donate money to a worthwhile charity. They must decide who or what to donate the money to and what they can do to raise that money. For now and for this exercise, they don't need the exact name of a charity, just a *category* of the kind of organization they want to help. The *category* can always be narrowed down to a specific place at a later time if the students are doing this as a real-life endeavor.

Tell the students that reporters use a few words to help them ask questions when they are working on their stories: who, what, when, where, why, and how. Let your students know that they, too, can use these same words to formulate questions that can help them make certain decisions.

For example, when the students ask themselves, "Who can we help? What can we do to help? How can we help?" they are establishing a *category* of worthy causes—perhaps animal shelters or organizations that aid other kids or provide disaster relief.

Allow the students a few minutes for discussion as you observe and listen. When the pupils share their thoughts, what resources or experiences did they use to determine the "who or what?" Younger students might say, "I saw a commercial for animals that need help. Could we help animals?"

Older students may be able to pose questions with a little more analysis and specificity: "Could we help people in our town or other kids who live here?"

Or maybe your students are familiar with a charity the school has donated to before, and someone might ask, "Should we do the same place we helped before?"

If the kids are stalled in their groups, try asking, "What would you like to *do* with the money you raise?" That might spark them into thinking of a category or people who need their help.

Once a *who* or *what* is named, it's time to decide how to raise the money. Let your students be as creative as they want, but advise them that their ideas must be sensible choices they could actually make happen. For example, if they want to have a car wash, is there a place they can do it? If they suggest a walk-a-thon, where would they walk and how far? Try to have them be as specific and logical as possible.

Is it possible for the students to see that this all began with questions they asked themselves?

ME, ME, AND ME

Needed: Prepared in advance: a three-column chart. Label the first column "Decision" and write down the various actions listed within this conduit. For the subsequent columns, use any icons, emojis, etc. that will be most relatable to your students and denote something positive for the second column and something negative for the third column. For example: thumbs up icon/thumbs down; happy face/sad face; yes/no.

Some of the most disagreement-inducing circumstances during a school day occur when kids accuse other kids—rightly or wrongly—of making decisions that affect others negatively: cutting in line, interrupting when others speak, always insisting that their idea is the only good idea, or, in more general kids' terms—being selfish and rude.

With proactive measures like teacher reminders and class rules in place, things can still sometimes go awry. Even mature fifth graders don't always make the best choices. However, seeing something in a cut-and-dried way might plant the seeds for making better decisions.

Try this exercise with your students, dividing the class into small groups. Tell the children that you need help sorting out which actions would be the best decisions to make and which ones would be the worst. Seeing how their peers categorize certain decisions might motivate some kids to be a little more introspective with the decisions they make.

In order to address all fourteen decisions, let each group tackle a couple of them. For example, Group A will discuss the first two, Group B the next two, etc. (If necessary, let more than one group address the same decisions.) The decisions listed here are suggestions, so please feel free to add others that are more germane to your classroom or school or select those that may particularly resonate with your kids.

DECISIONS:

- Cutting in line
- Making room for someone to sit
- My idea is always the best idea
- Waiting your turn to speak
- Singing weirdly in music
- Interrupting others when it's their turn to speak
- Listening respectfully to everyone
- Offering your extra pencil to someone who needs one
- Saying someone else's idea is yours
- Taking the seat someone else is headed for
- Giving back someone's dropped pencil instead of keeping it
- Making a disgusting face about someone else's lunch
- Picking up someone's jacket off the floor
- Holding the door for someone instead of letting it slam shut

After you organize the groups into which decisions they'll discuss, let the students classify their decisions into either the positive or negative column. Once the groups have decided which columns their decisions fall into, have them explain to the class why they categorized the actions the way they did.

Remind the students to be specific about why they put the behaviors in their particular columns:

- Did someone do that behavior to them and they didn't like it?
- Altruistic: The right thing to do?
- Are consequences driving their decisions?
- Is some behavior viewed as acceptable? "It's okay to interrupt when someone is speaking—everybody does it. It's okay if I make a face at her lunch."

For each decision presented, ask the rest of the class, "Do you agree with the group's choice of where that decision goes?" (thumbs up/down). Let the dissenters explain why they disagree.

WHAT'S IN A NAME?

Excitement may never be higher in a classroom than when there is an announcement that a name is needed for a class pet! If you've already engaged in this monumental decision-making task with your class or if you've never experienced it, go ahead and try this exercise in the spirit of practicing collaboration.

There are two steps for this prompt:

1. Before you do anything, explain that getting a class pet is a hypothetical situation—unless, of course, you do want to get one! Show your students pictures of four or five different animals you're considering; just for laughs, mix in one or two animals that would be totally outrageous as classroom pets, along with more practical choices. Select animals that have notable characteristics that would be familiar to your students.

Divide the class into small groups and ask, "Which animal would make the best pet for our class?" Once the pupils confer and decide (if no decision can be made, the majority can rule), let them present the reasons to the class why they chose the animals they did. When they offer their explanations, consider:

- Are their reasons practical? Did they choose the easiest animal to care for and feed? The one that would take up the least amount of classroom space? The least difficult to transport home for the weekend?
- Are their reasons emotional? An animal that is deemed the cutest or the loneliest might be reason enough for choosing him or her. Are these reasons as good or better than practical reasons to choose a pet?
- If the "just for laughs" animals were indeed chosen as the class pet, how did the students rationalize these choices? Ask them to realistically explain, for instance, "How would you take care of a rhinoceros in the classroom?" "Is there possibly a way?"

2. Once each group has chosen a pet, the name selection comes next. While there is often no rhyme or reason for the names we give our pets, for the purpose of making the kids think a little deeper and possibly have more fun, tell them that the pet's name for the animal they chose has to relate to its physical appearance or a unique characteristic that the animal is known for.

A simple example: If younger kids chose a goldfish as the class pet, they might name it Goldie. Older students may particularly like the task of connecting the name to a particular trait and might choose a name for a hermit crab that relates to its need to get a new shell as it grows.

It is possible that in some cases, one of the animals in the mix that you chose might have a unique characteristic that is also an important part of its physical appearance. The idea is to make it a little more challenging for the kids than just having them say, "We like the name Bob."

Let the kids brainstorm to come up with a name, and once all the groups have a name, let the students share them with the class. However, don't let the students explain which part of the animal's appearance or which characteristic the names relate to. Let the rest of the class think it through and guess where the name comes from . . . perhaps a hermit crab named Shelly?

TAKE ME TO YOUR LEADER

It can be a heartwarming experience for everyone when children rise to the occasion and step in as leaders at crucial times.

Sometimes it's easier for a child to be a spontaneous leader than it is to play a formalized leadership role. To encourage leadership skills, we have line leaders and class presidents and everything in between. This can be a good experience for kids, and it can also make them think about the kinds of leaders they want to be and the types of decisions they should make.

To practice some of these decision-making skills, let your students put themselves in the position of being "Class Leaders." Divide the children into groups of three to five and tell them, "Your group has been elected as 'Class Leaders,' which is like being the rulers of the class. You can do whatever you want. Which decision would display the best leadership qualities for your group to have?"

    A. Making decisions that help everyone in the class.
    B. Making decisions that would be best for your group and your friends.
    C. Making decisions that would be best only for you.

After the students discuss the options within their small groups, have them present their decisions to the rest of the class. While it might appear that this answer should be a slam-dunk, remember not to underestimate the power that loyalty to their friends has for many children or the sparkling lure of using power for oneself might have.

Did any group choose *Option B, "Making decisions that would be best for your group and your friends,"* as the decision that displays the best leadership qualities?

- If so, do these students view helping themselves as a benefit to being in power?
- Do they think that loyalty to one's friends is more important than making decisions that will help everyone?
- Do some students think that, as a leader, you should be able to help your friends even if it means doing something that hurts others?

How did the students explain their rationale for choosing the best leadership decision, *Option A, "Making decisions that help everyone in the class"*?

- Why do they think a leader should make decisions that will be good for everyone instead of just those closest to him or her?

- What words do the students use to describe this decision?
- Does anyone see this as being the fairest choice to make? If so, is fairness a necessary quality for a leader?

Ask the students who chose *Option C, "Making decisions that would be best only for you,"* why they chose this option. Also ask:

- Do they think that being in a position of power means they can think of themselves before anyone else?
- Do they think the people in their groups and those they would be ruling would question them about their "me" decision?
- If so, how would they explain that they would only make decisions that would help themselves?

This prompt can segue into a dialogue about how the decisions children make in their lives impact other people. You can ask, "Even though you are not 'Class Leaders' in real life, do the decisions you make affect other people? If so, how? If not, why not?"

For the last question set, present these choices to your students, asking them to select the best decision:

   A. Because you're the "Class Leader," you don't ever need to ask anyone else for suggestions or advice.
   B. You ask others for their advice and take it when you feel it is right.

Did anyone choose *Option A, "Because you're the 'Class Leader,' you don't ever need to ask anyone else for suggestions or advice,"* as the best decision?

- "What are your reasons for choosing this option?"
- "Do you think that asking others for suggestions is a sign of weakness?"
- "Can you think of any instances when a leader might have to ask for ideas or suggestions from other people? If so, what are they?"

A sagacious and objective leader is not a dogmatic one, so the students who chose *Option B, "You ask others for their advice and take it when you feel it is right,"* made the best choice. Ask these students:

- "How would asking for advice from others be helpful?"
- "Is asking for help and ideas from others a sign of strength?"
- "Would this be different from asking a friend to do your homework for you? Why/why not?"

When all the groups are done explaining their choices, give the students in the other groups a chance to agree or disagree with those decisions and explain their reasoning.

WHO SAYS I'M BOSSY?

A common complaint among school-age children, even ones in middle school, is that their classmates are "bossy." Often, the children who are known as the boss-in-chief don't see themselves that way. They think they're taking charge and making decisions for the common good. That can be true.

It can also be true that sometimes children think they have a monopoly on deciding how things should be and impose their decisions on everyone. That's when problems can arise.

For this conduit, tap into your students' kinesthetic and dramatic abilities as each group acts out a different scenario that revolves around making a specific decision. Some kids within each group will demonstrate bossy conduct, while others will illustrate cooperative behavior.

Divide the class into groups of four, five, or six children—whichever number works best for you. Each group will have a designated scene to perform and will be split into two subsets: a foursome would be divided two and two students, a group of five would be two and three, and a group of six would be split three and three. One subset in each group will act "bossy"; the other subset will act "cooperatively."

You can choose which subset will be bossy or cooperative, or the students can determine that. Explain the scenarios to each group, emphasizing that the partners decide how to act "bossy" or how to act "cooperatively." You may want to set parameters—no shouting, hands to yourself, and so on.

Tell the cooperative kids they will "take the lead," meaning that the scene will begin with them acting cooperatively to make the decision and solve the problem, and the bossy kids will step in and act out their bossy behavior.

Give the students a few minutes to chat with their partners so they can decide how they will portray their behaviors. Tell the students their performances should be short—maybe two or three minutes for each one.

Here are five suggested scenarios. Feel free to add others that may specifically reflect situations that occur in your classroom. If you need more than five scenarios for your groups, please duplicate one or more of the scenarios. Remind the students of their roles—some will be bossy and others will be cooperative.

PAINTING A MURAL
Your group will paint a mural on the side of the school building.

WHICH GAME TO PLAY?
Your group has to decide which game to play.

DECORATE!
Your group has to decide how to decorate the classroom walls.

THINK OF A NAME
Your group is in charge of creating a special class nickname.

SOMETHING FISHY
Your group has to decide what kinds of fish should be bought for the school aquarium.

Let each group perform its scenario for the class and then begin a discussion by asking the following questions.

For the bossy students:

- "What makes your actions 'bossy'?"
- "Can you give an example of how you could change one of those bossy actions into a cooperative one?"

For the cooperative students:

- "What makes your actions 'cooperative'?"
- "Can you give an example of how you could change one of those cooperative actions into a bossy one?"

Do any of the students equate their actions with compromising or not compromising? Which actions did they take to try get along with others? Which actions did they take to make it more difficult to get along? Did they contribute to solving the problem or did they put up stumbling blocks to making progress?

At the end of the discussion, ask:

- "What kinds of decisions do cooperative people make?"
- "What kinds of decisions do bossy people make?"
- "Is there a difference between the two? If so, what is it? If not, why are they the same?"
- "Did you like acting the way you did? Why/why not?"

Why Brainstorming?

The concept of brainstorming might seem a little counterintuitive because so much emphasis is placed on helping kids see that narrowing down their choices can help them make their decisions.

However, brainstorming is an effective vehicle that can kick-start the creative process and get ideas flowing. Eventually, these ideas will be narrowed down, tweaked, shined up, and twisted in all directions to accomplish the task.

Brainstorming can be used by individuals, but it is especially great in collaborative settings in which students can build on each other's ideas, connect them, discard them, and embellish them. The inherent spontaneous nature of brainstorming can project an atmosphere that's less scrutinizing and judgmental than more formal discussions. This can help the most resolute loners and the most reticent students feel more relaxed and less self-conscious about their contributions.

Kids can see the arc of their progress as they go from a blank sheet of paper and a bunch of unfiltered ideas to concepts that make sense and are logical and creative.

Chapter Seven

Don't Jump!

Even the most erudite and intellectual people can fall prey to making assumptions and jumping to conclusions. No one escapes them.

However, that doesn't mean we shouldn't try to impress upon children the importance of making decisions that are assumption free, based on as much information, evidence, and facts that can be gathered, and are not clouded by bias, prejudice, or what we think we know.

For any of the prompts in this section you can define an assumption in the simplest terms, as a guess for younger students, and as a theory for older ones. However you define it, be sure to convey that an assumption is an "iffy" proposition—it is something you admit to yourself that you are not sure of and it lacks facts, evidence, and proof.

IS SEEING BELIEVING?

Seeing something with your own eyes qualifies as the truth and prevents you from jumping to conclusions. Or does it?

Run this scenario by your students and *see* what they think:

You are at your friend Malcolm's house playing with some of his toys. You know that Malcolm and your other friend, Otto, play together too. You're surprised to see that Malcolm has a certain super hero figure. Just the other day, Otto told you that he's missing that same figure and can't find it in his house. It's certainly weird that Malcolm is playing with a toy that Otto can't find. There's only one explanation for this:

    A. Malcolm took Otto's toy.
    B. Malcolm did not take Otto's toy.
    C. Maybe Malcolm took Otto's toy. Maybe he didn't.

To open this discussion, start by asking the students which option they chose, and tally their choices.

Encouraging children to make clear-headed decisions can sometimes be at odds with the thinking that's needed to avoid rushing to conclusions. Kids' perception of reality can often be distorted or shaded by what they think they know or what they think will be. It can be difficult for them to recognize the possibility that there might be facts or evidence they're not aware of. Throughout the course of a school day, there are many opportunities for kids to jump to conclusions without having any facts or the full story.

Therefore, seeing Malcolm play with the same toy that Otto can't find might be proof enough for some kids to assume that Malcolm took Otto's toy. This kind of thinking can lead some students to choose *Option A, "Malcolm took Otto's toy."* After the students defend their reasons for choosing this option, pose these questions:

- "Is seeing Malcolm play with the same toy that Otto can't find enough of a reason to be *sure* that Malcolm took it? If so, how does this prove Malcolm took the toy?"
- "Can you show some proof, facts, or evidence that Malcolm took Otto's super hero figure?"
- Someone might say, "Well, it doesn't *seem* like Malcolm would have taken it." Is this a fact or a feeling?

You can also ask, "Do you have any of the same toys as your friends?" Students could argue that, while they do have the same toys as their friends, this is different. Why? Because Otto just lost the same toy that Malcolm has now. For this argument, you can ask, "Is it possible Malcolm already had his toy before Otto ever got his?"

Students who chose *Option B, "Malcolm did not take Otto's toy,"* are also making an assumption, just as their peers did in Option A. What are their reasons for saying they know Malcolm didn't take it? Some kids might respond, "Well, I have a feeling that Malcolm wouldn't do it." You can ask a similar question to one you might've asked the students who chose Option A: "Is a feeling a fact?"

Explain to your young minds that, despite wanting to think the worst of Malcolm, (Option A) or the best of him (Option B), they still don't have any proof that would support either choice.

While *Option C, "Maybe Malcolm took Otto's toy. Maybe he didn't,"* may appear as a wavering choice, it is the most sensible one. It doesn't jump to a conclusion or make an assumption. Students who chose Option C are acknowledging that there isn't enough proof to make a judgment about Malcolm one way or the other.

How do the students defend their reasons for choosing Option C? Look for some thinking along these lines:

- It's a coincidence that Malcolm has the same toy.
- Malcolm could indeed have had his toy long before Otto got his.
- Otto lent Malcolm the toy but then forgot that he did.
- Otto forgot to bring the toy home the last time he was at Malcolm's house and Malcolm is planning to return it to Otto the next time he sees him.

You can also ask, "Can making assumptions (or guesses) and jumping to conclusions affect the truth? Why/why not?"

If you still have time, stretch your kids' thinking by asking, "What information could the story have given you that would've made you think that Malcolm *did take* the toy from Otto?" "What information could the story have given you that would've made you sure that Malcolm did *not* take the toy from Otto?"

SCRUMPTIOUS!

It has happened to everyone: Someone uses a word you're not familiar with or says something you don't understand. You slightly nod, pretending that you know what they're talking about.

Anyone who has driven in a car with kids knows that they can pose an infinite number of complex, intricate questions in a short amount of time. Yet there certainly are times when children don't want to admit that they don't know something. Fear of "looking stupid" is the biggest culprit for remaining silent, especially if a child thinks that everyone else understands what is going on or knows the meaning of something.

This story shows what can happen when a pertinent question isn't asked. It will foster the idea that posing a thoughtful question instead of assuming something is a sign of intelligence . . . not an indication of weakness or stupidity.

One day, when Sally's grandma was visiting, she asked, "Sally, what is your most scrumptious food?" Sally wasn't sure what scrumptious meant, but she thought it might mean disgusting. Sally can't stand peas, so she told her grandma that her most scrumptious food was peas.

Sally's answer seemed to surprise her grandma, but she smiled and said that she had to go shopping. At dinnertime, Sally's grandma presented her with the biggest bowl of peas she had ever seen. "Enjoy, Sally!" she said. Sally felt sick to her stomach, but she ate the peas anyway.

After the story has been presented, ask your students, "What is the biggest mistake Sally makes in this story?"

A. Not asking what scrumptious meant.
B. Not liking peas.
C. Not knowing what scrumptious meant.

When the students defend their reasons for choosing *Option A, "Not asking what scrumptious meant,"* as Sally's biggest mistake, do the words "assumption" or "guess" factor into their explanations?

In Sally's case, her assumption caused her to eat something she didn't like and miss out on her grandma's special treat.

You can extend your students' thinking by inserting some hypothetical assumptions: Ask your students what would happen if you began teaching a new math lesson, then changed your mind and said, "I guess all of you know how to do this already, so just start answering the questions."

Or ask them what would happen if the principal assumed everyone knew how to get out of the building and they didn't need fire drills? Reiterate to your students that if they don't know something, anything—a word someone uses, directions, anything at all—they need to ask questions. A ton of questions! They will save themselves a lot of trouble, and they will get smarter!

Sally's biggest mistake is not *Option B, "Not liking peas."* While pea farmers and some parents may not agree with this, it's not Sally's fault she doesn't like peas. Everybody doesn't like something.

Your students know that no one can possibly know the definition of every single word in the dictionary, so *Option C, "Not knowing what scrumptious meant,"* also can't be Sally's biggest mistake. This answer pairs with the explanation for Option A: Sally's error in judgment wasn't that she didn't know what scrumptious meant but that she didn't bother to ask what it meant.

FAIR OR UNFAIR?

Situations that revolve around being "fair or unfair" can dominate a child's day. The list of infractions that populate a kid's world from their classrooms to their living rooms is endless. And in a kid's mind, something perceived as unfair is just as valid as something that is truly unfair.

There are times when the kids are right: some things are definitely unfair. As you teach your students to stand up for themselves, you can also show them that thinking in practical ways can help them decide whether or not their claims of unfairness have merit or if they are just assuming something is unfair.

See what they think of this story:

Three boys are carrying different things to the beach. The boys are all the same size and look like triplets. Matt is hauling one shopping bag stuffed with snacks; Roy has a beach chair and two beach towels; Jamal is toting a beach bag filled with books.

When the kids arrive at the spot their dad picked out, they dump their stuff on the sand. As they put on their suntan lotion, Roy grumbles, "You guys are so unfair! My stuff was heavier because I carried three things, and you each carried only one thing."

But then his brothers yell back, "Are you kidding? We aren't being unfair!" "In fact, we're very fair!"

Ask the class, "Who do you agree with: Roy or Jamal and Matt?"

To begin, ask the students who agree with Roy to defend their thinking. Do they, too, assume that three things must be heavier than one thing? What other reasons do they give for agreeing with Roy?

Do some students agree that Jamal and Matt are being fair? Do they argue that it doesn't matter how many things you carry—it depends on how much the things weigh? These students are venturing beyond the superficial appearance of the situation by assessing it and thinking logically about it.

Some kids might take Roy's flawed numbers theory and turn it around so they think Roy is the unfair triplet. The books inside Matt's shopping bag and the snacks in Jamal's beach bag would add up to many more items than the three things Roy carried. Yet this argument still begs the question, "What matters more? The number of things carried or their weight?"

End on a note of reflection: "Have you ever felt you were being treated unfairly at first but then realized you weren't? What made you change your mind?"

Trying to have kids think practically and logically when they are emotionally charged is challenging. Sometimes a conversation has to wait until nerves aren't so frayed. But teaching children to train a realistic lens on a perceived unjust act can help them make more astute decisions about whether or not they're being treated unfairly.

Or it can help them see that they've mistreated someone else. This can be an arduous path, but it can result in calmer, less stressed out kids who realize that they have been treated fairly. On the other hand, this same thinking and assessment can be invaluable when there is indeed an egregious injustice that must be looked at further by adults.

HOW DOES YOUR GARDEN GROW?

Hopefully, most of your students have some type of chores to do at home. While these tasks might be a pain for your students (and involve constant negotiations with adults), we know how important they are to foster responsibility, create a sense of family, and imbue a sense of pride for a job well done.

Have your students pretend that their job at home is to water the garden. Explain that they must make sure that the flowers and vegetables get all the water they need, *and* they have to do it in the *shortest* amount of time. Which route would they choose?

- A. Watering the garden is boring. It hasn't rained lately, so it will probably rain sometime soon. Don't water the garden. Wait until it rains, and your job will be done!
- B. There is a garden hose in the backyard, but you don't like using it because it's slimy and muddy. There is also a watering can, but you would have to fill it up in the kitchen sink. That means going in and out of the house several times to water the garden. But the good news is you wouldn't have to touch the slimy, muddy hose.
- C. The garden hose is certainly slimy and muddy, but it is right there in the yard, and all you would have to do is unwind it and spray the vegetables and the flowers.

Despite the fact that the hose is yucky, *Option C, "The garden hose is certainly slimy and muddy, but it is right there in the yard, and all you would have to do is unwind it and spray the vegetables and the flowers,"* is the most efficient, least time-consuming option and will ensure that the flowers and vegetables get all the water they need. And there aren't any assumptions!

When your students describe their reasons for choosing Option C, see if they can go beyond such answers as "It just seems quicker." You can ask, "Why does it seem quicker?" See if they justify that, even with the unwinding of the hose, it still wouldn't take as long as multiple trips with the watering can.

Option A, "Watering the garden is boring. It hasn't rained lately, so it will probably rain sometime soon. Don't water the garden. Wait until it rains, and your job will be done!" might be the Tom Sawyer answer, but it is not the best choice.

When your students defend this decision, they may claim that at some point, the garden will still get watered. Remind them that one of the requirements in the directions is that the garden had to be watered in the *shortest* amount of time.

So while it might be true that the garden will get watered at some point, it could be days, weeks, or longer before that happens. Ask your students, "What would take the shortest amount of time to water the garden: waiting for it to rain or unwinding the hose and spraying the flowers and veggies?"

In addition to Option A not getting the job done in the shortest amount of time, it's a no-no for another big reason. It's based on the assumption or a guess—not a fact—that it will rain soon. Even if it does rain soon, it is unknown how much rain would fall. A slight sprinkle could still leave the garden without all the water it needs.

You can also emphasize that waiting for the rain to tumble from the sky is walking away from the responsibility of being the garden's caretaker.

The longest option is *Option B*, *"There is a garden hose in the backyard. But you don't like using it because it is slimy and muddy. There is also a watering can, but you would have to fill it up in the kitchen sink. That means going in and out of the house several times to water the garden. But the good news is you wouldn't have to touch the slimy, muddy hose."*

The mere fact that this option has so many words in it may be the reason why some kids will choose it. Sometimes the only logic kids will employ in making a decision is selecting an option that sounds good because it has a lot of words. Did some students choose Option B because it was the wordiest?

And some students may have chosen Option B to avoid the slime and the mud. But ask them how that decision matches up with the directions that they must select the option that would get the chore done in the least amount of time?

This would be an opportune time to slip in a few words about the importance of listening and reading carefully.

RACE IN THE PARK

Read this poem to your students or let them read it, reminding them that they should listen/read carefully.

Race in the Park!

When the bell rings, off you go,
Fast, medium, or just plain slow,
You can hum, whistle, or even sing
But don't you dare do a thing
That rhymes with the words talk or sun,
But please, oh please, do have fun!

Then, after the reading is done, ask your students, "How will you get to the finish line?"

A. Walk
B. Hop
C. Run
D. Skip

The students who chose *Option B, "Hop,"* or *Option D, "Skip,"* will prove to be especially careful readers or listeners and will explain that they chose those options because they were the only activities that didn't rhyme with *talk* or *sun*, per the poem's instructions. They will also not have immediately jumped to the conclusion that this was a running race.

Whether the poem was read aloud or the students read it to themselves, the temptation is strong to focus on the question "How will you get to the finish line?" and disregard these two crucial lines: *But don't you dare do a thing / That rhymes with the words talk or sun.*

The inclination for most kids would be to choose Option C, *"Run."* Because their experience tells them that most races are running ones, it would be easy for them to assume that they would run in this race too. Unless, of course, they paid attention to the qualifying lines.

If your students chose Option C, explain to them that assumptions are often made because someone insists that they "know" what to do, even though they have not gotten all the facts or ignored specific directions.

For the students who chose *Option A, "Walk,"* which rhymes with talk, stress the importance of how tuning someone out or swiftly reading something can lead to misunderstandings and misinformation.

Even if every student chose *Hop* and *Skip*, this is a good time to explain that jumping to conclusions, making assumptions, and disregarding the facts can cause people to make decisions that are often not the best choices for them.

Take this further by sharing a personal experience of what happened when you made a bad decision based on an assumption or you made the wrong choice because you didn't listen carefully to someone. Maybe after hearing your example, your students will share their own stories.

At the end of your discussion, refer back to the poem and let your students think creatively about what other activities could propel them to the finish line. Kids will have fun thinking about jumping, crawling, leaping, biking, taking giant/baby steps, pogo sticking, wheeling, skateboarding, and so on.

If you have a few extra seconds, let them imagine themselves doing this race with an activity of their choice. If you're brave and have the space, you can let them perform some of their less rambunctious suggestions.

WHAT'S INSIDE?

Needed: Three containers, such as a salt container, box of crackers, and a cereal box, or three similar containers whose contents can't be detected from the outside. Leave one container with its insides intact—it can be a new, closed container or one that's already been opened. Completely empty the second container. Remove the contents of the third container and fill it partway with something other than what it professes to be. The filling can mimic the sound of the original contents when the container is shaken, or it can be something that would produce a totally different noise.

Also prepared in advance a three-column chart with the columns labeled according to the types of containers you have; the rows should be labeled "Empty," "Same Contents," and "Something Else."

This prompt will encourage students to think about how they arrive at their own decisions or conclusions and help them realize that relying on their own observations and common sense is a better choice than guessing or making an assumption.

Begin this prompt by holding up the three containers, but don't say a word. Casually walk around the classroom, shaking the containers and making sure they are visible to the kids, without letting them touch the containers.

After this short parade, refer to the chart and explain that you'll be doing a tally vote for the containers. When you hold up each container, ask:

- "Is it *empty*?"
- "Does this have the *same contents* that it's supposed to have?"
- "Is it filled with *something else*?"

After the tallying is completed, pose specific questions: "If you said the salt container is empty, how do you know that?" "If you said something else is in the Cheerios box, what could that be, *and* how do you know that?"

Let the kids explain how they came up with their conclusions and justify their decisions with lots of details. Their reasons might be factual: "The box of crackers isn't opened, so it must have crackers." Their reasons might be based on perception, correctly or incorrectly: "I think you smiled at the Cheerios box, so it must have something else in it." Perhaps a classic jump to conclusion: "The salt container was jangling, so marbles have to be in there." "Would marbles jangle?"

After the students justify their reasons, ask them if they could categorize their choices:

Were they based on facts? Assumptions or guesses? Evidence? Feelings? Experience? Observations?

Take a couple of minutes to pass the containers around and let the students shake them and examine the outside of the containers, but don't let them open them. Then ask, "Has anyone changed his or her mind about what's inside? Why/why not?"

- Was a closer examination of the containers enough to make some kids realize their initial choices were correct or incorrect? Have them explain their answers.
- Did using facts and observations help the students make some correct initial choices?
- Are certain decisions now seen as quick jumps to conclusions or assumptions?

- Was there anything the students could have done differently to make better decisions about what was in the containers? If so, what could that have been?

When the discussion is done, show the kids what's inside of the containers. Aha!

Chapter Eight

Huh? What Did You Say?

At first glance, it might seem odd that a slew of peculiar, even nonsensical expressions can help kids think before they make certain decisions. Yet the idioms in this section are but a few of the many sayings that can be handy tools to teach children the best practices for thinking.

In their funny and ridiculous way, these expressions can help deconstruct the reasoning behind practical and logical thinking. Using idioms as the basis for thinking prompts is also an easy way to integrate these rich and enriching little gems into your students' everyday vernacular.

For additional activities, you can have drawing materials at the ready and ask the students to illustrate any of these prompts or have them draw their own imaginative scenarios for any one of the sayings.

BETTER SAFE THAN SORRY

There are many qualities that can be identified as ingredients for being a "great teacher," and one of the most important ones is being able to have your students relate to you and to see that you are "human."

A good way to begin this exercise is by sharing a personal anecdote of something that happened to you when you left something important at home—either as an adult or as a child. (Kids love hearing stories about their teachers when they were kids.) Then ask your students, "Have any of you ever forgotten to bring something to school?"

A chorus of "Yes!" will echo in the room as many students will identify with this experience. Some kids forget something every day; for others, it is a rare occurrence, but it is bound to happen to everyone at some point.

Ask your students, "Which option could be the best solution to this problem?"

A. Hope your memory improves.
B. Before you go to bed, write down all the things you'll need tomorrow, and in the morning, check the list and make sure you have everything.
C. Tell an adult in your house to make sure you have everything you need.
D. Realize that everybody forgets stuff. It's no big deal.

Option B, "Before you go to bed, write down all the things you'll need tomorrow, and in the morning, check the list and make sure you have everything," is the best solution to the problem.

What were the students' reasons for making this choice? Does anyone mention that it is the most practical or responsible decision? If so, why? Do they see it as a worry-saver—meaning that if they use a checklist, they won't have to sit in math class wondering if they've packed their recorder?

Do some kids describe their own versions of "Better Safe than Sorry?" as they explain their reasons for choosing Option B? If no one brings up this line of thinking, ask your students if they know what this idiom means. If not, in basic terms, explain that sometimes doing something ahead of time to in a way "protect" themselves—being "safe" (making the list and checking it)—can help avoid difficulties later on—"being sorry" (consequences of leaving home without necessary stuff).

How did students who chose *Option A, "Hope your memory improves,"* defend their thinking? You can tell them that you, too, hope for things from time to time, but you know that hoping is not a way to solve a problem. Show them that by taking real steps on their own and thinking in a practical way they can avoid a troublesome situation.

Why do students who chose *Option C, "Tell an adult in your house to make sure you have everything you need,"* think that is the best option? As you have invariably done before, repeat your mantra that parents are not responsible for making sure their children have all their gear. Emphasize that this is their responsibility and one important way they can help themselves.

A note home to the household adults or a reminder email can also go a long way in reinforcing this.

Option D, "Realize that everybody forgets stuff. It's no big deal," is certainly a truism, but it's not a good reason to keep forgetting things. Ask your students, "Is it better to form good habits when you're young or when you're older?" Remind them to give good, solid reasons for their answers.

The goal is to make your students see that self-reliance is an important part of growing up. Something as basic as being responsible for remembering what to bring to school is one small brick they can add to that path.

Ask the children if there were ever times when they "were safe and not sorry" or if there were times when they were "sorry and not safe." Then you can ask them, "What seems like a better choice: a few minutes of planning and preparation or consequences you don't want?"

You can extend this example by telling the class, "Please bring in any kind of sock to school tomorrow." If you want, linger a minute or two, silently acknowledging time to let the students write this down in their assignment pads. It will be curious to see how many students bring in the sock.

A brief discussion the next day could be held: explanations from those students who remembered to bring in the sock and what helped them remember to do this; explanations from those students who forgot to bring in the sock and why they forgot to bring it in.

THE EARLY BIRD GETS THE WORM

Everyone procrastinates, and kids are no exception. Sometimes a decision to procrastinate is a maneuver to dodge something that's unpleasant, frightening, or challenging.

And sometimes kids decide to delay taking action as a default mode: The task or situation at hand, while important, isn't significant enough to be a priority—it can always be dealt with later. But sometimes choosing to wait until "later" ends up with disappointing results.

Similar to the prioritizing required for good time management, making a decision to act sooner rather than later can make the difference between kids having a chance to get what they want and letting certain opportunities slip away.

For this conduit, explain to your students that, at the end of the prompt, there's a phrase they might not be familiar with. Tell them you want them to think about what it could mean. Begin with this story:

One day, the principal announces, "Student assistants are needed to help run the activities at the school fair. Sign up sheets are in the cafeteria for anyone who wants to help. We only need a few assistants for each activity."

Corey can't wait to be an assistant for the water balloon toss! But when lunchtime arrives, there's a long line at the sign up table and he doesn't feel like waiting. He says he'll sign up another day.

The next day, the principal says that volunteers are still needed. But the sign up line is long again, and Corey decides to do it tomorrow.

But the next day, the principal exclaims, "Thanks to all who signed up! Every activity is filled, and we're ready for the fair!"

Corey is surprised and disappointed. When his friend, Martha, asks which activity he volunteered for, he says, "I wanted to do the water balloon toss. But it got filled."

Martha explains that that's the activity she's doing. "Joey and I signed up the first day, and two other kids told me they signed up the second day. I'm sorry you missed it, but you know, the early bird gets the worm!"

Ask your students what "The early bird gets the worm!" means. If no one has a satisfactory definition, explain that if you wait too long to do something (getting the worm), you could miss out on it because someone else decided to do it sooner and got there first (the early bird). In this case, the other kids made a sage decision to sign up quickly and got the volunteer job they wanted.

Let your students know that being the "early bird" doesn't always guarantee the results they want. However, choosing to take action and get an early start gives them a better chance of getting what they want.

Ask your students, "Did anyone ever 'get the worm' because you acted quickly?" "Did anyone miss out on 'the worm' because you waited too long?"

As always, give an example of your own dillydallying or worm success story in which your early action led to accomplishing what you wanted.

DON'T BITE OFF MORE THAN YOU CAN CHEW

The adage "If you want something done, ask a busy person" is a popular saying that's been attributed to two disparate people living in two different centuries: Ben Franklin and Lucille Ball.

There are those who argue that what Mr. Franklin and Ms. Ball have espoused is true. They are right. Others, however, argue that this isn't always true. They are also right.

The experiences of those in the latter category might derive from the idiom "Don't bite off more than you can chew." See what your students think when you present this prompt:

You love being busy and doing lots of different things. You play soccer and have a part in the school play. Once a week, you volunteer at your library and help shelve books. You feed your aunt's cats when she is out of town.

Your soccer team just got in the tournament, so there will be more practices. Well, that's good . . . maybe. It's taking more time to memorize your lines for the play than you thought, but you can do it. Oh yeah, there's that social studies project that's due soon. How'd that come up so fast?

One Saturday morning, you're overwhelmed about all the things you have to do and are worried you can't do them all. When you complain to your older brother about not having enough time to get everything done, he says, "Maybe you bit off more than you can chew."

What? You weren't even eating anything.

Before you ask your students what they think the idiom means, ask, "Is there something you could do differently in the future so you don't feel so overwhelmed?"

    A. No, if you like being busy, stay busy, even if you're overwhelmed.
    B. Yes, count on other people to do some of the things you said you'd do.
    C. Yes, you could cut down on the number of things you do.

Let's start with the most reasonable choice, *Option C, "Yes, you could cut down on the number of things you do."* When defending their reasons for this choice, some students may, by default, explain what the idiom means. If this happens, run with it and let them share their definitions. By selecting this option, your students are choosing to avoid feeling overwhelmed and are being realistic about their capabilities. When they explain their reasons:

- Do they think there's a difference between "being busy" and feeling they "can't handle" all the things they have to do? If so, what is that difference?
- Does anyone say that doing too many things might result in not doing anything well or not enjoying what they're doing?
- Does anyone say that, although they may not be able to do everything they want to do, that is still better than feeling overwhelmed?
- Can the students articulate how they could eliminate certain activities in the future? (Do only what they enjoy the most?)

You can also ask the students who chose this option, "Should you cut down on what you're doing if you aren't overwhelmed, worried, or complaining?"

Some students might view *Option A, "No, if you like being busy, stay busy, even if you're overwhelmed,"* as the most sensible choice because they won't have to decide which commitments to keep and which ones to eliminate.

These students might prefer being overwhelmed to giving up something they like. You can refer to two of the same questions you asked the students who chose Option C: "Is being busy different than feeling you can't handle everything? If so, what is the difference?" "Is it possible that by doing so many things, you might not enjoy them, or do anything well?"

How do the students defend their choice of *Option B, "Yes, count on other people to do some of the things you said you'd do."* This option is appealing because it allows the students to keep their full slate of commitments, while calling in reinforcements when they need them.

But Option B portrays a scenario that goes beyond everyone's occasional need for help. To have your students think more, ask them, "Should you tell someone that *you* will do something, even though you know you may rely on someone else to do it?" "What happens if you assume other people will step in for you, and then they can't or they don't do a good job?"

When all the choices have been defended, see if the discussion helped the students determine what it means to "bite off more than you can chew." In simplest terms: "Don't take on more than you can handle."

DON'T COUNT YOUR CHICKENS BEFORE THEY HATCH

In between the successes and setbacks that occur in children's lives are the adults who want them to reach for the stars, yet want them to know that they may not always grasp them.

Instilling confidence in children while having them be realistic about specific outcomes can be a thorny situation. Present this prompt to help your students see that they can be enthusiastic about something and full of self-confidence while still having realistic expectations.

Vivien is certain that she will win the school essay contest this year. She came in third last year, and she's positive that she'll win this time.

The theme "Who Do You Admire the Most?" is an easy question for Vivien: She admires her grandfather more than anyone she knows.

After she writes her essay, Vivien shows it to Gramps. He has a wide smile on his face, and thanks Vivien for all the kind words she has said about him.

"Just you wait and see, Gramps," Vivien says. "I'm going to win this contest and the prize money! I've got it all planned out. I'll save most of the money, but I'm going to use some of it to take you to dinner!! I've told everyone I'm going to win, and I've already written my acceptance speech."

Gramps stretches his eyebrows to the top of his forehead, looking surprised. "Well, young lady," he says, "I must say that your essay is well-written and nicely organized. And it's flattering to me, which I appreciate. I'm glad that you are brimming with self-confidence, but don't count your chickens before they hatch."

Begin the discussion by asking the students, "What does Gramps means when he says, 'Don't count your chickens before they hatch'?" Let the students share their opinions, but if none of their definitions hit the mark, explain that it means you shouldn't count on something good happening (having chickens) before it happens (hatching) . . . because it might not happen.

Then pose this question: "Is there something Vivien should or shouldn't do?"

    A. Vivien should enter the contest; she might win, but she should be prepared that she might lose.

B. Vivien shouldn't enter the contest because Gramps really doesn't think her essay is good enough.
C. Vivien should enter the contest and count on winning because she knows her essay is really good.

Ask the students who chose *Option B, "Vivien shouldn't enter the contest because Gramps really doesn't think her essay is good enough,"* if they can point to any proof that Gramps feels this way. Is Gramps just being realistic that other kids might also have excellent essays?

Did anyone choose *Option C, "Vivien should enter the contest and count on winning because she knows her essay is really good"*? If so, ask those students, "Now that we've discussed what Gramps means, do you think 'Don't count your chickens before they hatch' applies to Vivien?" Ask them to explain their reasons for their thinking and then ask these questions:

- "Is there any evidence that Vivien will win . . . or lose the contest?"
- "Does it make sense for Vivien to assume she'll win and make plans based on that assumption?"
- "Is there a difference between thinking positively ('I think I can . . . I think I can') and 'counting on' something to definitely happen? If so, what is that difference? If not, why not?"

Lastly, *Option A, "Vivien should enter the contest; she might win, but she should be prepared that she might lose,"* is the most reasonable decision for Vivien because it allows her to preserve her self-confidence while having realistic expectations. If Vivien wins, she'll be happy. If she loses, she'll undoubtedly be disappointed but will spare herself a bigger disappointment than if she counted on winning.

- Does anyone use the words "realistic, sensible, practical" when describing why they chose this option?
- Ask the students if they think that the kind of thinking used for "not counting chickens before they hatch" could help them in their lives. If so, how? Could it hurt them? If so, how?
- Do some students say that, by preparing herself for losing, Vivien avoids making an assumption?
- Do the students think they can still have self-confidence and challenge themselves to do things even if they "Don't count their chickens before they hatch"?

You can extend your students' thinking by asking, "Is there a difference between planning ahead for something and 'counting your chickens before they hatch'?"

Chapter 8

HASTE MAKES WASTE

Today's children live in a hectic world with the words "Hurry Up!" reverberating at every turn. Trying to get kids to slow down can sometimes be at odds with the frenetic pace they've become accustomed to.

Read this poem to your students and see what they think about rushing through things.

HASTE MAKES WASTE

I have a new household chore
To wash the kitchen floor.
Of all the jobs I've ever had,
It's not that terribly bad.
And I modestly admit,
I'm really good at it!

But today, there's so much else to do,
Including giving the dog a shampoo.
Will I ever get it all done
In time to have some fun?

A brilliant thought just came to mind
I know how I can leave this work behind!
I'll get rid of all that dirty grime
By washing the dog and the floor at the same time!

I'll need two buckets to do the cleanup,
One for the floor and one for the pup,
Scrub the kitchen here,
Rinse grubby paws there.

I don't want to boast,
But this idea may be my most
Cleverest yet—I'm a genius . . .
Whoa—doggie pal, what's the fuss?

His bushy tail
Knocked over one pail,
Then the other,
Oh brother, oh brother!

Now, he's got the mop—he thinks it's a bone
Hey, buddy, leave that alone!
Oh no! this isn't fair—
He's dragging that mop everywhere.

My oh my, I must confess,
That I've never seen such a mess!

Soapy puddles and gloppy mud,
It looks like some weird kind of flood.

Perhaps I never should have tried to be so quick
With my clever little cleaning trick.
I was trying to do things in a flash
But wound up with a lot of splish and too much splash.

My mother's words ring in my ear,
"Haste makes waste, my darling dear."
Such sound, wise advice—is really great
It's too bad that I remembered it too late.

Ask the class, "What does 'Haste makes waste' mean?" If no one gives a clear definition, explain that rushing through something (haste) can result in causing problems that will take longer to fix (waste) than if the task was done in a normal amount of time in the first place. This causes a waste of time and energy.

Then ask these questions:

- "Do you think the narrator senselessly rushed through his or her chores? If so, what choices could the narrator have made instead so she or he didn't wind up with such a mess at the end of the poem?"
- "If the narrator thought out this idea more, is it possible she or he would have realized that washing the floor and a dog at the same time could cause a big problem?"
- "Could planning out an idea in your head help you think of the possible problems that rushing through something can cause?"

At the end of the discussion, ask your students, "Did being hasty ever cause you to waste your time?" As always, chime in!

TWO HEADS ARE BETTER THAN ONE

Needed: Chart paper to write down the four items listed in the conduit; drawing paper, crayons, colored pencils, markers.

Tell your students that this thinking exercise is also an experiment, but that you'll explain that part later.

Let the students know that they'll be working alone for the first few minutes. Then they'll be paired with a partner so they can finish the project together. They'll be sharing their thoughts and ideas to solve a problem.

The intent is to have the students compare and contrast what it's like thinking by themselves and thinking with someone else on the same project.

Not all partnerships will be successful in coming up with a solution, and some students may balk at having to work with a partner.

However, in an effort to have your students practice the crucial concept of collaboration, the thought behind this prompt is "Two heads are better than one." At the end of the experiment, the students can discuss whether or not they agree with the meaning of this idiom.

Our class will be getting a special robot for the day. The problem, however, is that the robot is not yet a robot. It is a very large, real pumpkin, sitting outside the school building. The pumpkin will get her special powers and transform into a walking, talking, thinking robot the second she enters the school. Once she is inside the school, you can program the robot to do whatever you want and have fun with her!

However, if the pumpkin drops on its way into the school, it will break and will not be able to transform into a robot.

Explain to the kids that their thinking challenge is: "How can you and a helper get the pumpkin into the building without dropping it and breaking it?"

Write down the items below and tell the students that these props can help them get the pumpkin into the building. Any item or a combination of the items can be used:

1. A big shovel
2. A gigantic rubber band as tall as you are
3. A wagon
4. A large, soft, fuzzy blanket

Give the students a few minutes to work by themselves, having them illustrate and/or write down their ideas. Remind them that they will have a partner to help them finish up the project.

Then match everyone up with a partner. Tell the students that they must explain their idea to their partner, and they must comment and ask questions about their partner's idea. The ideas may be fully formed or in the beginning stages. Remind the kids that their ideas must make sense and be practical. The kids can use a couple of different routes to wind up with a solution:

- If both partners agree that one of their ideas makes the most sense, they can use that idea or tweak it, if necessary. If it is a partial idea, they can develop it further together.
- They can combine their ideas to design a solution they both like.
- They can forget their own ideas and create a brand new solution together.

It's possible that only a few partnerships will have formed a complete solution in the allotted time. The main thing is to see if the kids have made some progress in their decision making and collaboration and in appraising their ideas.

For those students who have discovered a solution, or at least a partial one, have them present it to the class. Their explanations must be specific: "How does the pumpkin get into the building by using a shovel and a wagon?"

Also ask the students to chronicle the steps they went through to arrive at their solutions: Did they use one of their ideas, combine them, or start over from the beginning? "I came up with _____, but then my partner _____. And then _____."

After the kids have described their solutions, ask everyone:

- "Did working with a partner make it easier or harder to solve this problem? Please explain."
- "Was it more fun to work with a partner than working alone? Why/why not?"
- "You knew ahead of time that after a few minutes, you'd have a partner to work with to help solve this problem. How did knowing that you'd be working with a partner make you feel?"

For those students who didn't make *any* progress with their partners, ask, "What could have helped you and your partner make some progress?" (More time? More flexible thinking?)

Now, explain to the students that the experiment part of this project was to see if they liked working by themselves better than working with a partner. Ask them:

- "Have you ever heard the expression, 'Two heads are better than one'?"
- "What do you think that means?"
- "Do you agree with this? Why/why not?"
- "Is it always better to work with someone else? Why/why not?"
- "Is it always better to work alone? Why/why not?"

Some children steadfastly prefer to work alone, so not all of them will agree that "Two heads are better than one." Maybe by doing this experiment some light can be shed on why they don't like having a partner. Although some children (as well as adults) may not prefer it, working with others is a necessary life skill.

If there's time, ask the students what they would like the robot to do or present that question to the class as a collaborative activity for another day.

Chapter Nine

How Did This Happen?

As the nineteenth-century American essayist, philosopher, and poet Ralph Waldo Emerson said, "Shallow men believe in luck. Strong men believe in cause and effect."

That effect, in essence, is a consequence. However, when consequences are viewed through the prism of a child's mind, anything goes.

Sometimes the more practical, sensible choice wins out, not because it's appealing, but because it's more appealing than the obviously dreadful consequences. At other times, a child's attraction to the least sensible decision is stronger than his or her misconception that the consequences "didn't seem that bad."

Then there are instances when the aftermath of an ill-conceived decision blindsides the most astute-thinking kids because for some unknown reason, the word *consequence* didn't enter into their minds. They never registered that ten-second thought: "If . . . then . . . ."

The conduits in this section focus on the role that consequences—negative and positive ones—can play in making decisions . . . underscoring that cause and effect go hand in hand and are not isolated from each other.

OH, THAT LITTLE VOICE

Read this riddle-poem to your students as an introduction to a discussion on what happens when clear-headed decision making takes a back seat to temptation. Before you begin reading, tell your students that the last word in the poem is missing. Ask them to listen carefully so they can shout out the final word, which rhymes with the last word in the line before it:

Chapter 9

Oh, That Little Voice

You probably think that I was wrong,
And that I should have been strong
And thought it through,
But what could I do?

I tried to tell myself, "Leave it alone" —
"It's not your phone!"
I only played one game, honestly,
For maybe two minutes . . . maybe three.

Yes . . . I know the phone isn't mine,
And everything was perfectly fine
Until the phone slipped and dropped
And then, astonishingly, plopped
Into the goldfish tank
And sank, and sank, and sank.

It's not all bad, Dad,
Please don't look so sad.
I suppose you're not interested in my advice,
But I've heard a wet phone dries out nicely in a bowl of rice.

Whoever would have guessed
That I'd be in such a mess?
It was that crackly, little temptation voice—
It gave me no other choice . . .
It should definitely take the blame,
'Cause it kept whispering, "It's just one teeny little game!"

But now, it's clear to me,
And I see . . . I really see
That if I hadn't lost my senses,
I wouldn't be facing these _____ (consequences)!

After the poem is read (you may want to read it a second time), ask your students, "Who or what does the narrator first blame for his or her decision?" (temptation).

The narrator points out two things in the poem, one in the beginning, and one toward the end: "But what could I do?" "It (temptation) gave me no other choice." Ask the class, "Is it true that the narrator didn't have another choice instead of playing with the phone?" "If so, what was that choice, and how would that have changed what happened?"

See if the students have any suggestions for what the narrator could have done to avoid giving in to that little voice. Examples include: think ahead to the consequences; do something else to take his or her mind off playing with the phone.

Ask the class if the narrator's decision to play with the phone—and to play near the fish tank—put him or her in the position of having to face unwanted consequences. Does the word irresponsible come up, especially with older students?

Some kids might counter that the only thing the narrator should have done differently was not to stand near the fish tank. To these students, you could ask, "Should the narrator have made the choice to take the phone in the first place?"

To think further, ask the kids to think this through:

- "Let's say the narrator received permission to play with the phone, and it still slipped into the fish tank. Did the narrator make a thoughtless decision to play near the tank?"
- "Was it bad luck that the phone fell?"
- "Do you think that the consequences would be the same if permission were asked? Why/why not?"

You can also ask for personal stories (yourself included) of how sound reasoning won out or lost to temptation.

WALKING THE DOG

You can begin this conduit by asking, "Do you have any responsibilities for a pet at your house?" Have your students describe those responsibilities and then ask them a couple of basic questions, such as, "How often do you do this chore?" "Do you like doing this? Why/why not?"

If you have a classroom pet, let the students discuss their responsibilities for that pet.

Once this has been done, present this poem about Diana, who is supposed to walk the family dog. Before you read it, emphasize that close attention should be paid to the choices that Diana thinks she has. For younger students, you may want to read the poem a second time. You might also want to point out that the choices are not labeled A, B, and C, but instead are found in Diana's words within the poem.

Walking the Dog

It's my job to walk Nate,
And that's usually great!
But today, in this dreary rain,
It's going to be such a pain.

Should I wait for it to stop?

> *(But then I might have to use a mop!)*
> *Without any bit of doubt,*
> *I should really take Nate out.*
>
> *But if I hide long enough under the bed,*
> *Somebody else will take him out instead.*
> *What's that I hear?*
> *A leash jangling, loud and clear . . .*
>
> *Yes! My sister is walking the boy,*
> *Such happiness! Such joy!*
> *Uh oh . . .*
>
> *My mom is calling a name . . . mine.*
> *And that's not a very good sign.*
> *I guess I'll be doing some talking*
> *About why I skipped the dog walking.*

After the poem is read, ask your students if they can tell you which three choices Diana thinks she has:

- *Should I wait for it to stop?* (And then take Nate out.)
- *I should really take Nate out.*
- *But if I hide long enough under the bed / Somebody else will take him out instead.*

Once the class has outlined Diana's choices, discuss them in the order they were described, starting with *Should I wait for it to stop?*

For those students who chose this option, their reasons may very well focus on the fact that to them, it would be easier to walk a dog when it's not raining than when it is. And while this makes perfect sense on one hand, see what they think after you ask them: "Would you rather walk Nate in the rain or clean up a big mess in the house?"

Do the students understand that Diana realizes there might be a consequence to this decision when she says, *"But then I might have to use a mop!"* (Kids will think this is disgusting—enough to deter them from choosing this answer?) Here are some other questions:

- "It might be easier for you to walk Nate when it's not raining, but is it easier for him to wait until you want to walk him?"
- "Is it fair to Nate, who relies on you for his care, to make him wait?"
- "What if it doesn't stop raining for hours?"

You can then ask the class, "Do you think Diana is being responsible to Nate if she waits for the rain to stop?"

When Diana says, *"I should really take Nate out"* she is making the most responsible, practical, and considerate decision—not only for Nate, but also for herself. Are your students' rationales for choosing this option based on practicality—easier to have a soggy walk than a disgusting clean up? Emotion—not wanting to be mean to Nate? Or just wanting to stand up to their own responsibility? Something else?

And lastly, there is the unfortunate choice that Diana made: *But if I hide long enough under the bed / Somebody else will take him out instead.*

The flaws in this decision reflect those in Diana's choice to wait for the rain to stop: shirking responsibility and unpleasant consequences. You can ask:

- "Did Diana do her job?"
- "Is Diana's mom happy?"
- "What do you think will happen because Diana didn't walk Nate?"
- "When we make a decision, should we think about the consequences?"

When discussing the consequences that can be caused by actions or inactions, can any of your students articulate the connection between making impractical choices and the consequences they can have? (For example: Waiting for the rain to stop and having to mop up the subsequent mess.) Sometimes thinking about the ensuing consequences is enough to nudge a child (or adult) in the direction of the right choice.

WHO DID IT?

To quote the famed author and editor Norman Cousins, "Wisdom consists of the anticipation of consequences."

After you present the excerpt and the related options, let your students explain why they chose the options they did.

You're playing with a toy on the kitchen table, which you're not supposed to do. You know the usual consequences for disobeying family rules: early bedtime, privileges taken away, or somehow making up for doing what you did.

But now, really, you're just playing with a toy on the kitchen table . . . until the toy leaves a deep scratch the size of the Grand Canyon right in the middle of the table. OH NO!

What should you do?

- A. Put a book over the scratch to cover it up.
- B. Walk away from the kitchen and pretend nothing happened.
- C. Tell the adults in your home what happened, apologize, and see what you can do to make up for scratching the table.

In the interest of being honest and owning up to responsibility, *Option C, "Tell the adults in your home what happened, apologize, and see what you can do to make up for scratching the table,"* is the best choice. It is also the most practical choice, although some of your students may not see it that way. What was the main reason your students chose this option?

- Did anyone think that telling the truth might bring about a reprieve or soften the consequences for disobeying the family rules?
- Did anyone choose it to get the consequences over with?
- Was Option C selected because it was "the truth and the right thing to do"?
- Is there merit in owning up to something sooner rather than later?

If your students chose some of these reasons, they might have been thinking emotionally, but maybe, without even realizing it, they were thinking practically too. It is possible that their promptness in telling the truth may result in less punitive consequences, and by owning up to their mistake early on, they won't waste time and energy wondering when someone will discover the scratch.

Choosing *Option A, "Put a book over the scratch to cover it up,"* and *Option B, "Walk away from the kitchen and pretend nothing happened,"* undoes all the practicality that Option C offers. Yet their attraction is that some children will see them as a way to escape the consequences. Kids are often consumed with the here and now and often don't think to look ahead.

Let them think about how short sighted these options are by asking:

- "How long do you think it will take for someone to discover the scratch? What will happen then?"
- "It might be hard to tell the truth in the beginning, but is that harder than pretending and acting as if you didn't do it?"
- You can end the discussion by asking, "Can thinking about consequences help you to make the right choices? Why/why not?"

If you have older students, stretch their thinking by reading to them the Norman Cousins quotation "Wisdom consists of the anticipation of consequences" and asking them what they think it means.

WE CAN

Needed: One two-column chart, labeled "Action/Cause"; "Consequence/Effect."

Consequences are often viewed in a negative light, but this prompt will help your students experience the good consequences that can come from their well-thought-out, constructive choices and decisions.

Tell your students, "Let's think of some ways you can help the environment. Because the world is such a big place, let's think of actions we could take in our own classroom and school that could improve the environment."

Begin by presenting the chart you've made or let the students observe as you write down the column titles. Explain what the columns mean: the *"Action/Cause"* column is where the students' ideas go (the actions they want to take) and the *"Consequence/Effect"* column is for how these actions will help the environment. Even second graders will be able to understand the columns once you explain them.

Emphasize to your students that their thinking will have two parts—for every *action* or *cause*, there has to be a particular *consequence* or *effect*. For example, "Run the bathroom faucet only when you're washing your hands" would go in the *"Action/Cause"* column. "Saving water" would be listed in the *"Consequence/Effect"* column.

However, point out to your students that their thinking doesn't have to follow one pattern. In some cases, they might find it easier to think of the consequences/effects first and then the actions/causes after that.

By establishing your school and the classroom as the parameters for the environmental concerns, you are showing your students that you are purposely narrowing down a vast field of choices into more manageable chunks. Watching you do this in various instances may help your students internalize this behavior so that they, too, will begin doing it.

Additionally, having the students think in terms of their school and classroom gives them a close connection to the problem at hand and helps facilitate feelings of pride and ownership.

When you ask the students for their ideas, they might begin by shouting out "Let's save electricity!" "Let's save water!"

When open-ended suggestions such as these are offered, have the students add more clarity and specificity to their thinking. For example, you can say, "Saving water and electricity are great ideas to help the environment. Does anybody have *one way* we could save water while we're in school?" "Does anybody have *one way* to help us reduce the amount of electricity we use?"

In addition to the ideas your students come up with, you can ask some basic questions to help them to think harder and possibly open the doors to more ideas. Sometimes it is the simplest queries that thrust the thinking gears into motion and produce amazing results:

- "Are there ways that we *waste water or electricity* in school?" Thinking of a solution in these terms might result in some actions that could *save water* and *electricity*.

- "Can anyone think of how we can begin recycling in our classroom or improve how we recycle?"
- If recycling is currently in place, "Do you ever toss something in the garbage instead of recycling it?"
- "What can we do to encourage people not to litter on the school grounds?"

Look around your classroom to see if there are ways to encourage some creative alternatives: "Is there something we could use rain water for instead of running the tap?" "Could we store something in that big empty box?" The kids will love feeling resourceful and helpful.

As the students present their ideas, have the rest of the class assess them to ensure they are sensible, practical actions that can be carried out: *"Yes"* for "Don't flip on the water fountain faucet just because you're walking down the hall." *"No"* for "Let's drink less water from the drinking fountains."

When all the ideas are charted, ask, "What can you learn from this chart?" Do your students see that even kids their ages can execute change for the better by making decisions that will have good, positive consequences?

Let the students decide where to hang their chart and what they should name it. It can be a daily reminder for them of how they can help the environment, and it can remain an inspiration to see that what they do can indeed have positive consequences.

YOU NEVER KNOW

Needed: Chart for recording students' comments.

Some decisions, made with high hopes in mind, don't always turn out the way they were imagined. But that doesn't mean that something positive can't come out of them.

More than anything, Iola wants to be an actor when she grows up. She always gets the lead part in the school plays.

On Monday morning, Iola sees a flyer at school: "The Main Street Theater is presenting "Annie." Auditions for the role of Annie will be held on Saturday at 10:00 a.m."

Acting in her school plays is great, but auditioning for the Main Street Theater? Scary, but double exciting!

Iola couldn't think of anything else all day except whether or not she should audition. When she told her parents about "Annie," they said, "It's up to you if you want to audition." When she asked her older sister what she should do, she said, "I'm not you. You decide if you want to audition or not."

Iola was annoyed because she didn't want to make the decision herself. She wanted someone to say, "Do it!" "Don't do it!"

All week long, Iola asked herself whether or not she should audition. It made her nervous just thinking about it.

At this point, take a break from reading and ask your students *what* they think Iola should do and *why* they think that.

    A. Iola should audition.
    B. Iola should not audition.

Remind the students to use the word "because" when they explain why they chose either Option A or B. For example, "Iola should audition because she might get the part" instead of "It's a good idea for Iola to audition."

Write down the students' reasons on the chart and resume reading.

By Saturday morning, Iola decided to audition. There were many other girls trying out, but Iola did her best. She was called back for a second audition, and by now, Iola had told everyone that she auditioned.

Then Iola found out that she didn't get the part.

Iola's family and friends were upset for her, and at first Iola was disappointed. Then something changed. When her sister asked her how she was feeling the next day, Iola said, "I'm okay. Something good came out of this experience."

Ask those students who thought Iola should audition if they still think that way, even though they now know she didn't get the part. Refer to the reasons they gave before. Are their reasons still the same? If so, why? If not, how are their reasons different?

Reread the part where Iola declares, "Something good came out of this experience." Look at the chart responses and ask, "Could any of *your* reasons be the good consequences Iola means? Why/why not?"

Do any of the positive consequences include the pride Iola could feel from making her own decision or challenging herself to audition, even though it was scary? Some students, especially older ones, might see that Iola's not getting the part could be a good experience because that's what happens to real-life actors.

Ask the students who felt that Iola should not have auditioned if they still feel that way and to explain their thinking. Refer to the reasons they offered before. Do the students still have the same reasons? If so, why? If their reasons are different, how are their reasons different?

You can also ask, "Is it possible that if Iola didn't try out for the part that she would always wonder if she could have gotten it?" "Is deciding not to audition a better choice than always wondering if she could have gotten the part? Why/why not?"

You can end the discussion with: "At first, Iola was disappointed that her decision didn't turn out the way she wanted. Then she saw that something good came out of it. Has something like this ever happened to you?"

As always, feel free to share your own story.

Chapter 9

IMAGINE IF . . .

Needed: Prepared in advance: Index cards with the "Actions/Causes" listed within this conduit. Make copies from these pages or hand-print the actions, cut them into strips, and fasten each strip onto a card. Choose one of the twenty-four "Actions/Causes" index cards for each team of two students. Please note that some of the suggestions toward the end of the list are geared toward older students. Feel free to let your imagination loose with your own unrealistic "Ifs."

For this conduit, let your students take a bit of a break from thinking practically . . . well, in a way. Divide the class into teams of two (and one threesome, if necessary) and distribute one index card to each team.

The students will soon see that the actions (causes) on the cards don't exist in the real world. Explain to them that their challenge is to be as creative as they can be and come up with consequences (effects) for each of these imaginary actions.

However, the consequences they think of must still make some kind of sense and relate to the actions. Read these two examples to the class: "If people barked instead of talking . . . *then* dogs would talk instead of barking." "If people barked instead of talking . . . *then* we'd never have homework again."

Ask your students, "Which example shows that the consequence is related or connected to the action of people barking?" Explain that using the word "then" can help them think of the consequences.

Encourage your students to fashion as many consequences as possible for the action they received.

- If humans could fly . . .

- If the world were made out of candy . . .

- If kids were bigger than adults . . .

- If you lived on another planet . . .

- If you could be homework-free forever . . .

- If you never had chores to do . . .

- If cars were never invented . . .

- If you were a toy instead of a kid . . .

How Did This Happen? 97

- If you could always do whatever you wanted to . . .
- If kids could become president . . .
- If dinosaurs still roamed Earth . . .
- If you lived with a giant . . .
- If you could eat whatever you felt like . . .
- If it never got dark outside . . .
- If the sun disappeared . . .
- If everything was free at the stores . . .
- If humans were the pets, and pets were the masters . . .
- If you didn't go to school . . .
- If humans turned into robots . . .
- If everyone lived forever . . .
- If no one ever disagreed with each other . . .
- If we never had wars . . .
- If everyone had the same amount of money . . .
- If there weren't any computers . . .

Give the teams several minutes to come up with their consequences and write them down. Allow each team to share the actions (causes) and consequences (effects) with another team. When that sharing is completed, bring the class together and ask:

- "Did your consequences make sense and relate or connect to the action on your index card?"
- "How about the consequences of the team you were paired with?"
- "Can you make any suggestions to improve any of the consequences?"
- "Was this hard to do? Why/why not?"

- "Was this easy to do? Why/why not?"
- "Was thinking of consequences for imaginary situations harder or easier than trying to imagine consequences that could happen in real life?"

If you still have time, choose some of the actions you didn't give to the teams and offer them to the entire class, or ask the students to come up with their own imaginary actions and consequences.

CAUSE AND NO EFFECT

Needed: Optional chart paper.

A "consequence," as defined by the Merriam-Webster Dictionary, is "something produced by a cause or necessarily following from a set of conditions."

It's often hard to know why children act one way and not another. As adults, we encourage them to think through their actions so they are kept safe and healthy and can make prudent decisions. Invariably, though, every child will bump up against various kinds of negative consequences in their lives.

What if kids didn't have to confront unwanted consequences for certain behaviors? Maybe they can't escape getting a broken leg by jumping off a high wall, but what if they didn't have to worry about being grounded or having certain privileges taken away because their behavior was unacceptable, against the rules, or just plain inappropriate?

Conversely, what if they knew they'd be rewarded with good consequences every time they did something they were "supposed" to do?

Begin this prompt by asking, "Can anyone give us a definition for the word 'consequence'?" If you want, write down the definitions on the chart and have the students agree on the best definition, or let them craft an amalgam of the ones presented.

Once a consequence is defined, explain to the students that you don't want them to answer aloud right now, but they should think quietly to themselves about the following:

- "Do you try to think ahead of time how your actions will affect yourself or others?"
- "Think about the times you've made smart decisions because you knew there would be not-so-great consequences if you chose different decisions."
- "Think about the times you thought about unwanted consequences but went ahead and did something you shouldn't have anyway."

Sometimes asking a question geared to the "general universe of kids" instead of asking for individual responses encourages some kids to speak more freely, generating a more robust and richer conversation.

So to begin this discussion, tell your students that you're wondering how kids would act if they lived in a world where they could do whatever they wanted and they would never face any bad or negative consequences for their actions. Explain that you're not saying they're super heroes and will never get a broken leg if they fall out of a tree that they shouldn't have climbed.

Instead, tell them to think of the choices kids make that could normally bring about unwanted consequences. For example, not doing chores at home might result in lost privileges; lying to friends might wind up losing their trust.

But for now, in this pretend world, there aren't any negative consequences. The kids can do whatever they want. Whenever they want.

Ask for a thumbs up/thumbs down vote: "If there were never any bad consequences for their actions, how would kids act?"

A. I think that kids would still try to do the right thing.
B. I think that kids would do whatever they wanted, even if it meant bad consequences for someone else.

Ask the students who chose *Option A, "I think that kids would still try to do the right thing,"* why they think that kids would still behave the way they "should." If there aren't any bad consequences to worry about, what would make kids want to try to act appropriately? If someone says that it's important to "do the right thing," ask "What does doing the right thing mean?" "Should it be important to do the right thing?"

Remind your students that they don't have to give examples from their own lives if they don't want to, but they should still back up their thinking with general examples.

Have the other students explain why they chose *Option B, "I think that kids would do whatever they wanted, even if it meant bad consequences for someone else."* Then ask:

- "Do you think that bad consequences are the only things that kids think about when they choose their actions? If so, should they be?"
- "Should kids make choices that might be bad for others but good for themselves?"
- "What would the world look like if nobody had to face not-so-great consequences?"

For a different spin, ask the class:

- "Would kids change how they acted if they knew they'd be rewarded with good consequences every time they did something they were 'supposed' to do?"
- "If so, how would they change their behavior?"
- "If they wouldn't change their behavior, why wouldn't they?"

Chapter Ten

Words of Wisdom

From the Experts

Dedicated, brilliant, caring, astute teachers are not hard to find. That is not an assumption or a biased opinion. It is a fact. These educators are found in every pocket of the world, teaching anything and everything to everyone.

The knowledge and expertise of some of these educators are presented here as further suggestions on how to help children think, make decisions, and solve problems on their own. The educators interviewed have taught myriad subjects—from reading to art and philosophy to English as a Second Language. Their experience ranges from teaching children as young as two to graduate students. They've educated students in private and public institutions, stretching from Asia to New England.

MAKE IT SAFE . . . RELATABLE . . . OPEN . . .

One of the best ways to motivate students to think for themselves is genius in its simplicity. "Inspiring independent critical thought," according to Edgard Jason Rincon, "begins with creating a safe and inviting classroom culture built on mutual respect. I believe it is imperative that students challenge one another in meaningful ways so they might expose themselves to varying perspectives."

Rincon is a bilingual special education teacher–learning behavior specialist 1 for second and third graders at the Nathan Davis Elementary School in Chicago. When it comes to students voicing their own opinions, Rincon says there can often be "somewhat of a 'group think' mentality whereby a student may express thoughts he or she believes are the most commonly held by others."

To help students think on their own, Rincon presents information "that somehow touches upon the students' daily lives and interests, thereby attempting to create a bridge between their prior knowledge and the material that is being presented to them."

Dan Josephson (the author's son) taught English as a Second Language (ESL) at various grade levels in Taiwan and South Korea and feels that inspiring children to think on their own "is most effective when we do not bring them into our world, but rather take a step into theirs."

"When we ask students questions that relate to their daily activities, or personal hobbies, so much of the work is already cut out for them," according to Josephson, who is now an adjunct lecturer in Asian Studies at City College of New York in New York City. "Students will feel much more inclined to answer questions truthfully and passionately if they are about something they feel attached to."

In Ireland, at Maynooth University, Department of Education, Dr. Joe Oyler, lecturer in teacher education and former classroom philosophy teacher, echoes a similar sentiment: "Tap into what inspires them [students] already. I think making connections to what is meaningful or challenging in their current experience is a good way to tap into this."

An essential ingredient that's needed for students to think for themselves, according to Oyler, is "giving them the space and opportunity to do so." He finds "that students are quite ready to begin to think for themselves, but may not actually trust that we want them to. All too often, the questions they get asked are rhetorical or mean to assess student retention of information."

GOING BEYOND ... TAKING RISKS ... MAKING CHOICES ... MAKING MISTAKES ...

Getting kids to think—to really think—does indeed require teaching that surpasses rote, mechanical measures. Amy Ziebarth, head of school at the independent Far Brook School in Short Hills, New Jersey, says, "When we talk about progressive education here, we talk about the benefits of actively constructing one's own knowledge rather than memorizing content given by the teacher, which is often ephemeral and quickly forgotten."

Ziebarth says, "This independence and ownership over learning stays with students for life and can be applied to any job, any problem, any challenge."

A vibrant, thought-provoking educational atmosphere, as Ziebarth and others attest to, must be intentional and purposefully thought out. As Oyler further explains, "To build space for thinking, I try to create a classroom atmosphere that de-centers my role as the teacher, encourages risk-taking and provides time and structures for deep thinking."

A member of the executive board of the Institute for the Advancement of Philosophy for Children, Oyler engages his students in Community of Inquiry approaches, which can be used in philosophical as well as nonphilosophical contexts.

As he further explains, those within the Community of Inquiry take part "in collaborative, group argumentation, where reasons and evidence are generated and evaluated" by the participants. "Their contributions and questions serve as prompts throughout the process."

The risk taking Oyler mentioned is such a fundamental component of the philosophy at Far Brook that it is noted prominently in the school's statement of purpose, which, as Ziebarth points out, is "to create a supportive and caring community that cherishes love of learning, creativity, and individuality, and that provides the teachers and students with both support and freedom to take risks in order to reach their full potential."

Ziebarth further explains that "encouraging students to take risks is the first step to providing an environment conducive to independent thinking." One way Far Brook supports risk taking is by requiring student participation in a "large number of diverse activities"—choir, sports, theater, fine arts, playing instruments, and woodshop.

As an integral part of its approach to learning, risk taking is embedded in Far Brook's curriculum, which emphasizes choice and decision making. For example, Ziebarth explains that "our reading and writing curriculum values student choice in the topics they write about and the books that they read." In concert with this is the importance that Far Brook's teachers place on students' "thinking that extends and goes beyond what specific content has been taught."

By this, Ziebarth means, "Can they take what they've learned and apply it in a different situation? In a reading class a teacher might teach students about analyzing character through their understanding of a shared text, but student learning is assessed by seeing how a student can apply that skill in her own novel, with coaching at first, but ultimately on her own."

At the Warwick Valley Middle School in Warwick, New York, former art teacher Pam Swanson makes a comparable analogy. Swanson explains that when children learn about the color wheel and color theory, that is one stage of a process. The next step, however, is implementing that knowledge into a work of art.

"The students have to make a choice where to put their colors," she says. "A student might ask herself, 'Do I want that area to stand out?'" Then the student would draw on her knowledge, and might decide "to use complementary colors, for example—purple and yellow—to make that section pop."

Ziebarth describes independent thinking—thinking that necessitates the transference and application of new skills—as "messy, and will involve mistakes." And for this kind of thinking to take place, a special understanding between the teacher and the student must exist.

"Students and teachers must have a great deal of trust and share a mutual understanding that mistakes will happen, they are valuable, and are the source of the most important kind of learning," says Ziebarth. "This culture, this atmosphere, is what encourages independent thinking."

A firm believer in the concept that "Life is a choice—everything we do is a choice," Swanson feels strongly that "in order to build students' choice making skills, I had to establish confidence in them. The most important aspect for me was to instill a 'Yes, I can attitude' in my students. It is so important to believe in them. If you make them feel good about themselves, they'll have pride and confidence in themselves and make better choices."

To demonstrate her point, Swanson tells a story about an open-ended project for her fifth graders. The task was to "walk with a line" and design an imaginary creature. The students had to make various choices, including adding different textures and colors for the drawing.

When one boy finished his project, he stood on a stool, and shouted, "I can draw! Look at my drawing! I never knew I could draw!" That confidence, Swanson says, "leads kids to make good choices."

CONSTRUCTION PAPER... OXYGEN... PHILOSOPHY...

Hands-on projects can also help students with their thinking when words aren't forthcoming. As Deborah Richardson, a registered occupational therapist and former teacher, explains, "I have found that discussing preferences or opinions can be easier through different media."

Richardson, who taught kindergartners through third graders at Far Brook, says that asking children to tear pieces of construction paper into grassy strips can be the needed sensory distraction or tension reliever that enables them to think deeper and flesh out a tale about a nature scene.

While the students are tearing the paper, the teacher might suggest some animals that could live in this scene and then ask, "What else could be in the grass?" Richardson explains that "hopefully, while tearing the paper, the focus on the question will be less intense and the students' response more automatic—maybe to say a lion."

The teacher could ask additional questions, such as, "What might the lion be doing there?" Adding the use of chalk or painting materials could extend the project, and "hopefully the story will develop," says Richardson.

Another idea that Richardson has used to motivate thinking in the classroom also stems from her occupational therapist background. "If the group appears to be having problems with an assignment, movement can often help energize the thinking process."

She recommends bringing the group outside and having the children walk in a straight line, "imitate movement—hands high in the sky, out to the sides, stomping to a beat or clapping to a song."

If going outside isn't possible, "the children can stand next to their chairs doing similar activities with the ending being 'take your arms and wrap yourself in a hug and/or pat on the back.'"

According to Richardson, "With the increased stimulation of oxygen to the brain, hopefully increased thinking skills will occur."

What else stimulates independent thought? Well, according to Dr. Thomas E. Wartenberg, senior research fellow in philosophy at Mount Holyoke College in South Hadley, Massachusetts, and director of the website "Teaching Children Philosophy," it's philosophy.

When young children are engaged in philosophical discussions, Wartenberg explains that they are "stating a position, finding reasons that support their position, thinking about counterexamples to alternative positions, etc. This is really having them involved in the process of thinking for themselves."

Wartenberg, who is also a member of the Graduate Faculty of the Department of Philosophy at the University of Massachusetts–Amherst, teaches his students how to lead philosophy discussions with elementary school children.

His experiences with elementary school children led Wartenberg to incorporate "a similar component" into his college courses, although he "also had to be sure that the students were learning certain material. The crucial thing for me as a teacher was to do something that I had told elementary school teachers over and over again: They had to get out of the center of the discussion and let their pupils interact with each other by following the norms for a philosophy discussion."

When this happens, Wartenberg says, additional motivation isn't necessary to inspire students to think for themselves. "Just taking part in such discussion inspires them, for they really enjoy thinking through their positions in discussion with their peers."

Asking a simple question about ice cream can transform a classroom into a thinking lab.

For example, Josephson says, "We can catalyze such personal methods of thinking by asking a question such as, 'Who likes ice cream?' and there is a solid chance that a plethora of hands will shoot up. Students will then already be in a state of competition to share their personal opinions about ice cream."

This segues into "Which flavor is the best?" and finally, "But why?" "This now digs into the realm of philosophy, or backing up an argument, which is a huge step for elementary level students," Josephson says. "They have become engaged in the process of critical thinking, without the teacher having pressured them to do so."

Jennifer Esposito, a second-grade teacher at South Mountain Elementary School in South Orange, New Jersey, sparks her students into thinking for themselves by "giving them situations where they have to think outside the box in order to solve the problem. There may be no right or wrong answer or solution."

Giving students the time and space to explain how they have arrived at their answers or solutions is crucial. As Ziebarth explains, "Our math curriculum values problem-solving skills. Students are exposed to many ways to solve a problem. While there is never one right way to solve a problem, students learn that what is important is being able to think independently and explain how you reached your solution."

EXPECTATIONS ... ROUTINES ... ACCOUNTABILITY ...

To foster independent thinking in her first-grade class at Tuscan Elementary School in Maplewood, New Jersey, Cynthia Vengraitis reminds her students that "I am not supposed to be thinking for them" and that "they are in charge of their actions."

When Vengraitis asks questions such as "Is your mom in first grade?" it can gently remind a child of his or her own responsibilities. A request "to make a more sensible choice that works for everyone" can lead to a student plan of action instead of reliance on a teacher.

Like many other educators, Vengraitis's main focus for the year is having her students "be active, independent learners. From day one, our routine is in place and children are guided toward making choices about behavior and learning."

Vengraitis says that "once routines are in place, I pull back as much as possible."

The significant impact those routines have on independent decision making is also recognized by Rincon at Nathan Davis Elementary and Esposito at South Mountain.

"I encourage independent decision-making by making the students feel like they are an essential and important part of the classroom," Esposito says. In September, Esposito and her class create "a Class Expectations Chart for the year—so that we are all accountable—the students as well as myself. Everyone in the class signs it so that we are all aware."

That "understanding of classroom rules, expectations, and goals" is, according to Rincon, the process that activates independent decision making.

In Rincon's experience, "When students feel comfortable with the routine of a classroom setting and open dialogue in which their varying opinions are respected and taken into account, they are more likely to engage in the type of thinking that promotes autonomy in the classroom."

Rotating classroom responsibilities, such as being the line leader or door captain, can foster that independence, Rincon says.

When students "are encouraged to take control over their learning" and help the classroom run efficiently, Rincon says, they "feel more comfortable with their place within the classroom and the decisions they make to facilitate discussion, ensure that materials are being used appropriately, and engage interpersonally with one another."

Oyler tries "to invite them [his students] into the decision-making processes going on in the classroom. 'How should we spend this block of time?' 'I'm trying to figure out the best way to approach our project. What do you think the best way to proceed is?'"

When encouraging independent decision making, Rincon feels he must be "very deliberate." One way he does this is by "presenting scenarios to students in which they may have a moral dilemma about other student conduct and whether or not they should share the information with a teacher or other adult. With expectations clearly in place, students are more confident that their own decisions are the right choice."

SCENARIOS... HISTORY LESSON... GOOD PLANNING...

Josephson, too, has used scenarios and stories with his young students to help motivate them to solve problems or illustrate the effects of ill-conceived decisions. One such humorous story revolved around the consequences an overly stuffed Teacher Dan suffers from eating too many doughnuts.

Drawing the sequence of events on a dry erase board, Josephson would show "the progression of Teacher Dan's overeating, with his belly increasing in size, tears welling up in his eyes, and his face changing color." As the kids laughed, Josephson would ask, "Why is this happening to Teacher Dan, and what should he do next time to stop it?"

A story like this happily unleashed tons of student advice as well as jokes, Josephson says, but it was also a lesson that prompted student participation and engagement and made them think twice about the consequences of eating too many sweets!

A lesson of a different sort—one from George Washington—found its way into Ramona Sojacy's fourth-grade classroom at the Holy Family School in Carteret, New Jersey. Sojacy (the author's sister) "tried to teach my students that all choices have consequences, good or bad, and to think a situation through carefully before acting."

While at Holy Family, Sojacy often incorporated lessons from the academic curriculum to emphasize the importance of making good decisions. She points to George Washington's crossing the Delaware into New Jersey with the Continental Army in 1776 as a "good lesson on decision-making."

The linchpin of Washington's shrewd strategy for the Battle of Trenton was his plan to seize the British boats along the Delaware River's southern bank so they couldn't pursue Washington and his men. The general and his army deftly crossed the Delaware on Christmas night and surprised the unsuspecting Hessians.

Her students, Sojacy explains, "learned that as a result of this battle, the American forces began to have confidence that they could prevail in their battle for independence from Great Britain."

However, the knowledge accrued to Sojacy's students has traveled far beyond learning about a pivotal event in the American Revolution more than two centuries ago. Sojacy believes that "by the study of history, the class learned that good planning leads to actions that can have positive consequences and that they could apply these lessons to their own lives."

This attention to good planning and thinking ahead was also a key to success in Swanson's art room. For example, when working with clay, her sixth graders "had to sketch out what they wanted to make and explain what techniques they were using before they got the clay. They had to make good choices, and explain how they were going to make it work. For instance, they had to show what escape route they would have in place for the air to come out," Swanson says.

CONSEQUENCES ... PROMPTS ... DIALOGUE ...

Why is it so critical that an escape route was included in the students' planning? Swanson explains that without it, "The project wouldn't make it through the kiln firing process. It would blow up." So to avoid this catastrophe, "The students had to map the project out ahead of time, and know what their plan of attack was going to be."

Similarly, Rincon believes, "It is imperative that students be given the opportunity to devise their own plan when considering how best to tackle a problem or solve an issue. Students must be allowed to think through the various consequences that their decisions may have, and consider how these consequences may affect them both in positive and negative ways."

At Tuscan Elementary, Vengraitis has a similar mindset. She does not solve her first-grade students' problems, but she will "often talk them through solutions, frequently steer them towards helping themselves."

Telling the students "Let's think about it" and posing questions can help kick-start their thinking. For example, "Where do we usually put finished papers?" can be asked of a child who doesn't know where to place a paper. "How have others solved the problem?" and "What can you do about it?" are two other great stimuli Vengraitis uses to get kids thinking about how to solve their own problems.

In Rincon's special education classroom, "various sentence starters help to serve as useful prompts to motivate independent thinking and problem solving." Some of them are:

- Because I know ... about this topic, I think that ...
- When I think about this, I feel ...
- When I look at my notes, I find ... which makes me think ...
- The problem is ... possible solutions could be ...
- If I choose to ... the consequences might be ...

Prompts like some of those below are also important tools when Oyler's students engage in a Community of Inquiry:

- What are your reasons?
- How does that relate to our question?
- Is that true?
- Is this true in all cases?
- What are we assuming here?
- What is the consequence of believing this?
- What difference would it make in practice?
- What might someone who disagrees with you say?
- Have we come to this conclusion too quickly?
- Do we have enough evidence/reasons to draw this conclusion?

As the author of *Big Ideas for Little Kids: Teaching Philosophy Through Children's Literature* (Rowman & Littlefield Education) and the series editor of the upcoming book series *Big Ideas for Young Thinkers* (Rowman & Littlefield), Wartenberg suggests, "If you find a picture book that addresses a philosophical topic that you want your students to think about, having them discuss the picture book turns out to be a great way to get the students thinking for themselves about that problem."

Wartenberg, who is also the president of the Philosophy Learning and Teaching Organization, says that when he "added picture books into my college classes, students were able to get a better handle on what they thought about the abstract philosophical issues that are the bread and butter of philosophy."

In his elementary school classroom, Rincon encourages "dissent as a means of pushing students to find the value in their very own opinions and express themselves as valuable members both within and outside of our school community."

Josephson seconds that: "We never want our students to fight, but we do want them to engage in healthy disagreements or discussions." Starting a dialogue pertinent to students' lives "is an exciting and effective way to encourage them to think independently. We always want to talk as little as we can, simply lighting the fuse of the firecracker that will be independent student thinking and opinions."

INTERVENING ... RETHINKING ... KNOWING WHEN ...

There are times, though, when independent thinking, decision making, or learning isn't occurring for various reasons, with either an individual child or the group as a whole.

When should an educator step in and set a rethink? Many teachers would agree with Esposito that a tipping point "is when students become frustrated or there is a start to an argument."

For her first-grade class, Vengraitis "pulls everyone back to the carpet and announces, 'Let's clear up our confusions so we can do our best.'"

When various students in Rincon's class aren't able to answer a specific question, that "is a good time to reset potentially with a sentence starter, other oral prompts, or a lead to a particular decision."

After that decision is made, Rincon emphasizes, "it is then important to review it and briefly discuss why in fact this was the correct decision to make and the impact that the decision may have on our classroom."

Sometimes, according to Rincon, after "reviewing our mutually agreed upon and student created rules and expectations," a reset would come in the form of changing seating arrangements or desk positions to facilitate learning.

"The barometer in these instances is measured at the point in which behavior begins to present as a significant impediment to overall student learning," Rincon says. However, as vital as implementing a reset might be, "equally as important is a restorative discussion that follows in which students address why specific changes were necessary and how they were able to succeed in light of these changes."

For Oyler, the point of intervention is "when the process is breaking down." If Oyler sees "the group is losing focus on the guiding question/purpose of the inquiry, or if our procedures and processes of inquiry aren't being followed, then I will intervene to get the process back on track."

How and when to handle this delicate juncture of intervention is a distinguishing feature that defines the essence of teaching. "One of the things that makes teaching an art and not a science," says Wartenberg, "is knowing when you have to leave your role as a facilitator and start doing something more substantive. What I've found is that there are times when the discussion is really getting off track and no one in the class seems to be aware of that."

When this happens, Wartenberg "will step in to bring the issue back into the center of our discussion. But, I don't have a formula that someone can just adopt to do that. It really is something that one learns by experience."

Josephson, like others, agrees that educator interventions should be judicious and limited, but advises, "It is also still our job, of course, to step in and assist them, explain ideas, and improve the learning environment when necessary."

According to Ziebarth, one time that warrants stepping in is "when students are afraid of mistakes and risks." This, says Ziebarth, "takes affirmative teaching to help students understand" that mistakes are an important aspect of learning.

Another crucial time that Ziebarth feels requires intervention is "when students struggle with motivation. This is more difficult. In a school that values independent thinking it is challenging to know when to demand performance and how to respond to minimal effort."

Ziebarth further explains that "ultimately, when a child is suffering from motivational issues, we step in to provide a more structured learning environment that has less independence and more direction, with the plan to move them toward greater independent thinking."

If his students were "struggling to come up with answers, or the level of excitement seemed lower than expected," Josephson would ask more questions. "It actually becomes somewhat of a Socratic method," he says.

While the purpose is to "incite better answers," Josephson cautions that "it should never get to the point where I formulated their opinions. Instead, I pretended they have certain answers, so they feel the need to correct me."

For instance, if a student wasn't offering "a strong enough response, I might have pretended to assume a student's favorite food was Brussels sprouts—'Oh, I see! You love to eat Brussels sprouts!' The student may then say 'Ewwww! No way! I like pizza!'"

ROLE MODELING ... CONNECTING ... VISUALIZING ...

Since time began, teachers have devised ingenious ways to help their students learn. One tried and true strategy is role modeling, which can take various forms.

At one time, Wartenberg thought he could role model "by simply discussing philosophical texts and that students would pick up on what I was doing."

However, many students couldn't transfer what Wartenberg was doing "into their own intellectual practices."

So one way Wartenberg remedied this was to read the text "aloud sentence by sentence and ask the students to explain what was going on. Together we would discuss our understanding of the sentence."

This group connection is a critical and essential one that surfaces time and time again in discussions of learning, decision making, and problem solving. As Oyler explains, "I try to make my thinking transparent to students by talking through my thought process. I include why it was hard and how it felt to confront the challenge. I also model by including them in the process, as I think we should draw from others in support of making decisions, even personal ones."

Discussing decisions with his class is high on Rincon's list too, as he has shared some of his own decisions, from education choices to "choosing the right clothes to wear for a given occasion."

Consistently modeling how he solves problems has helped Rincon "in leading students toward addressing their own daily issues and working to find motivation for addressing these issues with confidence and a sense of resolve independently."

Esposito says that with her second graders, "I solve my problems aloud as well as model different ways to solve the problem. I have the students choose the way I should solve my problem."

Rincon also role models by illustrating how he would make a decision he knows his students encounter. For example, he might say, "I know that if I'm able to complete this assignment tonight, I can earn additional technology time tomorrow, so I will choose to wait to play my video game until later."

With his paraprofessional aide, Rincon will also role-play "how I might handle an issue where we saw misbehavior in the hallway, at lunch or outside during recess. These reenactments can very much help drive the point, especially among younger students."

Role-playing and constructing stories are "the best method" to explain difficult concepts to younger students, in Josephson's opinion. "It is our responsibility as educators to bring ourselves into the world of the age group we are teaching."

For example, a story about a damaged Transformer action figure can lead to certain questions: "'How can I help this Transformer? What happened to it? Well, here is what Teacher Dan would do . . . he would kiss it.' A purposely ridiculous solution like this should ignite corrective responses from the students, giving us insight into how they would solve the problem."

According to Rincon, providing his students with tangible devices is one more way to help them see that they can solve problems on their own. For instance, when working with small groups for a math lesson, Rincon's students use personal dry erase boards and manipulatives, which "provide powerful visual and spoken aids that demonstrate for students how to effectively read the problem, use our previously taught step by step process guides and ultimately arrive at a correct and defensible solution."

Rincon feels that "once students are able to visualize the process of decision-making and problem solving within the classroom setting, they are far more likely to not only employ these tactics but also create their own."

REAPING THE REWARDS . . . CELEBRATING . . . BUILDING CONFIDENCE . . .

Educators not only feel a sense of pride in their students when they make prudent decisions; some of them, like Vengraitis, "celebrate those making responsible choices, instead of calling out those who aren't." For Vengraitis, it's important to think aloud as she is solving her problems in the classroom. "I celebrate when I solve a problem, like moving furniture to create a user friendly traffic flow. I also talk a lot about how the students are grown ups in training."

As they move forward on that journey to becoming those grown ups, Vengraitis observes that when her students think, make decisions, and solve their own problems, "They go through their day with grace and dignity!"

Vengraitis reminds her students that other people will form opinions of them based on what they see. "They get to help others form those opinions by what they show to the world. I ask them who they want to be and what to do to become that person."

According to Josephson, presenting children with relatable material they are interested in also helps them think and act autonomously. This, in turn, increases their passion and engagement in classroom activities and helps them have a "more positive attitude" toward their academic studies. "The students are less likely to feel like they are completing an assignment or chore," softening the "work" aspect of "schoolwork."

For Rincon, "one of the great joys of the profession" is seeing "a child take hold of a sense of ownership over his or her own thoughts and individual academic processes." A boost in confidence and independence can help a child require less scaffolding and be more willing to finish an assignment independently instead of immediately following up with Rincon. These positive effects of autonomous thinking are even more wonderful because they go beyond the child who is reaping them.

"Students who have successfully made these decisions alone or solved problems independently" are, according to Rincon, "more likely to lead a classroom discussion or small group whether in language arts, mathematics or the sciences" and are "more likely to be the ones assisting others in their academic work, when appropriate, as they relish the notion of being a leader both within the classroom and the larger school settings and communities."

These students, says Rincon, "are also poised to continue growing as classroom leaders, which creates a bedrock for the leadership skills that will serve them so well throughout their social and professional lives."

With heightened confidence, says Esposito, so too comes the feeling for her students "that what they want to share will not be frowned upon. Also, I think that when students feel confident in their decision-making they are more open to criticism from their peers. They are able to support their decisions with evidence. When students feel confident, they are more willing to speak up and share ideas."

One handy tool that Esposito's students use is a graphic organizer from a unit on opinion writing called OREO: O: Opinion (food, movies, restaurants, toys, etc.); R: Reason for their opinion; E: Examples for their reason; O: Opinion restated.

"Once the kids learn the OREO, they continue to use it for other opinions on other concepts. It helps give them confidence in their opinions because they are able to support their opinions with examples and evidence."

The acquisition of increased self-confidence that comes with students thinking for themselves and solving problems on their own "leads them to live more fully," says Wartenberg.

"Since all of my techniques involve having students work together," Wartenberg explains, "an important result is that the students start to see their peers as resources, as genuine partners in the search for knowledge and truth. This leads to much deeper relationships among the students, both at the college and elementary school levels."

One shining example of this occurred at the Martin Luther King Jr. Charter School of Excellence in Springfield, Massachusetts, where Wartenberg's students lead philosophical discussions with the children. A teacher who was on playground duty "witnessed an altercation among the second graders. She was about to intervene when she heard one of the children say to the other children, 'Wait! We're philosophers. We know what to do.'"

"What they did was to allow each of the participants to share their point of view, much as we do in our classroom sessions. This led to a discussion and, after that, the dispute was resolved and the children went back to playing with each other."

This, according to Wartenberg, illustrates "that children learn a style of dispute resolution from philosophy discussions where, after all, people do have different views and enter into discussions in hopes of resolving the issue."

As for the future, Rincon sums it up this way: "With the knowledge that employers often seek both collaborative and independent decision-making skills and abilities, it is my firm belief that all educators and administrators would be well served to very deliberately include sections within unit plans dedicated specifically to developing the skills needed for independent thought, autonomous decision-making and thoughtful/comprehensive problem solving skills."

Chapter Eleven

Food for Thought

A Menu for Educators

Kids aren't the only ones who can become stymied by the decisions and dilemmas that face them every day.

Their dedicated teachers, too, contend with decisions and actions that not only affect themselves but also the students who mean so much to them. For many teachers, the best part of their day is being with their students in their classrooms, engaging and helping them learn not just about subject matters but about life.

Teaching, admittedly, is not done in a vacuum. Every teacher's pedagogy is informed by relationships with colleagues and administrators, and keeping those relationships copacetic and collegial is invaluable to everyone.

The prompts in this section are meant as food for thought. While they may not exactly reflect the dilemmas and problems encountered in your school, hopefully you can take away some ideas that can be helpful in similar situations.

LEAVE IT ALONE

Just as students are cautioned time and again about the effects and consequences of their actions, sometimes educators must take a step back, too, before acting.

Let's say that some teachers have been talking disparagingly about another colleague. You're new to the school and haven't met this person yet, so you don't have anything to say.

In a couple of weeks, you find yourself on the same committee as this teacher. To your surprise, you find her pleasant, helpful, and tremendously devoted and caring to her students. You are tempted to:

A. Go to the teachers who spoke disparagingly about her and tell them what you think about her.
B. Ask her if she realizes there are teachers who speak negatively about her.
C. Ignore what others say about her and base your relationship with her on how she treats you.

As everyone knows, the most well-meaning intentions can backfire, causing consequences and events that no one imagined. Situations like this one are best left alone, as your feelings will be known by your actions toward this person.

OUTSIDE THE COCOON

Educators can be thought of as solitary creatures, drawn to teaching because they like establishing an individualized rapport with their class, watching their students evolve and grow over the course of a school year.

In a way, being in a classroom with students is similar to being in a cocoon or in a self-sufficient little city. This is in contrast to the other work teachers do: collaborating with colleagues in meetings and committees.

Sometimes it's beneficial to be reminded of the types of decisions teachers would hope their students would choose in the spirit of collaboration:

- Think about the common goal, not an individual one.
- Recognize that everyone is entitled to his or her opinion.
- Stick to the issue at hand.
- Accept that everyone is in this together.
- Don't take anything personally: agree or disagree with someone because of the issues, not personal feelings.
- Think of your role: What can you do to bring people together?
- Assess the stumbling blocks: What can be done to get around them?
- As progress is made, take a minute or two to acknowledge each small step that is made, making the group feel more cohesive and more in tune with each other.

IN MY OPINION

This prompt may be familiar territory to anyone who has had a personal and professional relationship with a colleague.

A particularly sensitive issue comes up at a faculty meeting, with many people chiming in with various opinions and no consensus. You think that one of your closest friends and colleagues at school thinks the same way as you do. However, based on his comments during the discussion, you realize that you are on opposite sides of the issue.

You decide not to weigh in on the matter at this meeting, but you know the issue will be taken up again at another time. Your friend, who assumes you agree with him, tells you that he is surprised that you didn't speak up, voice your opinion, and back him up.

You can:

A. Tell him you disagree with him and explain your thinking.
B. Give him a bland response about why you didn't speak up, skirting the fact that you disagree with him.
C. Decide that the issue is not worth your friendship. Tell him you agree with him and that you'll speak up at the next meeting in his defense.

While they would counsel their students to avoid the two more convenient, "easiest for the moment" responses (Options B and C), some adults would decide to choose them. These options do take care of the problem . . . but only momentarily, and they can cause a more uncomfortable situation in the future.

WHAT DO I REALLY THINK?

Even the most poised, articulate educators can be caught off guard when asked by a superior for their input on a particular subject.

Whether the setting is a colleague-filled meeting or a one-on-one consultation with an administrator, there might be mitigating factors as to why you're not sure if you should really offer your opinion. It could be that you feel you still need additional time to gather more information and facts to back up your opinion.

Maybe you know that your opinion differs wildly from those of the majority of your colleagues, and you're not sure if you should stir up controversy.

Perhaps, as a seasoned school veteran, you're aware that your viewpoint is in sharp contrast to the one held by many of the newer teachers. While you stand by your opinion, you don't want to alienate those teachers or appear that you are not "forward thinking."

Maybe you're one of the newer teachers and you're afraid to say what you think because you're not sure how your superior or the rest of the faculty will respond to your forthright comments.

On the other hand, maybe you're hesitant to reveal your opinion because you know it's in direct opposition to what your superior wants to hear.

Trusting yourself and those around you has a lot to do with how to handle a situation like this. If you feel that you need more time to evaluate the issue to support your opinion fully, say so, with the caveat that you'd be willing to give your honest opinion later, no matter what you feel the consequences may be.

Your superior may somehow know that your opinion is vastly different from your colleagues, and she or he wants to make that opinion known. It's possible that your contrary opinion needs to be put on the table not to stir up controversy but to help create progress in the group's thinking by offering a viable perspective that's not apparent to many people.

As a seasoned teacher, your point of view may be out of step with the newer teachers, but that doesn't necessarily mean that it's not "forward thinking." If you believe in your opinion and the positive impact it can have, it doesn't matter what others think as long as it's offered in a respectful, collegial manner. Perhaps your superior asked your opinion because it is valued, no matter where it falls.

Adults, like kids, might be hesitant to propose their opinions when they are the newest or the youngest. A new teacher being asked by a superior to speak up in front of everyone or one-on-one might not feel confident enough to say what's on his or her mind, but this is an opportunity to show how you think and why you think it. Everyone may not agree with those thoughts, but the more open-minded, astute-thinking peers will respect you for saying what you believe.

If your opinion does clash with your superior's, that was the chance your superior was willing to take. Maybe you should take it too.

COUNTERPRODUCTIVE

Educators spend lifetimes teaching their students to think before they act and not to jump to conclusions and make assumptions. Yet sometimes that advice is hard to follow, even when it's about yourself. Or maybe especially when it's about yourself.

It can be your first presentation to parents or your millionth. You are:

A. Overly confident that all will be perfect.
B. Somewhat nervous, but you know you're prepared.
C. Assuming the worst: There will be questions you can't answer, any technology you might be using will go haywire, and your nervous eye twitch will resurface.

While a realistic, happy medium for many people would be to be a little nervous but comforted by knowing they are prepared, everyone has his or her own way of dealing with these situations. However, ask yourself, "Is assuming anything—either way, positively or negatively—ever productive?"

GETTING FULL

Teachers view themselves as doers—those who effect change and make things happen.

While these are admirable and worthy traits to have, sometimes they can become a teacher's worst enemy. For dedicated, concerned educators, it's often hard to say "No," whether it's to being on one more committee or presiding over a school-wide project. New teachers may want to show how much of a team player they are and pile on as much as possible.

Seasoned teachers may like having the reputation of being the one who gets everything done. If, however, somewhere along the line "biting off more than you can chew" sounds too familiar, ask a few simple questions before you volunteer for the umpteenth time:

- Do I really have the time for this?
- If I do this, what will it take time away from? Is it worth it?
- How will I feel if I say "No" to this?
- How will I feel if I say "Yes" to this?

WRONG FOOT FORWARD

It's one of those things. Someone says something at a meeting; you say something else and instinctively you know you've gotten off on the wrong foot. This happens to everyone, and if you're like most people, this will be uncomfortable and disconcerting.

A choice to ignore what happened for now might provide a much-needed cooling off period or a laying low time to avoid making a bigger deal out of it.

Choosing to speak to the other person and try to smooth things over is another possibility. This might be a more intuitive decision: You'll probably feel it in your bones whether or not you should try to smooth things over. Either way, a wise, pragmatic choice is to make a commitment to yourself that the next encounter with this person will be better.

CUT IT DOWN

Sometimes adults, like children, have too many choices. A little rethinking can go a long way toward cutting down a cumbersome number of ballooning options into a few manageable ones. Judiciously narrowing down a field of choices can help make any decision easier to make.

Imagine that you want to redo one simple, tiny aspect of your classroom. As you start thinking, you let your focus wander and now a million other ideas are exploding inside your head—not solutions to remedy the original problem but ideas for other things in the room that have unexpectedly grabbed your attention.

Instantly, the issue you set out to remedy has taken a back seat to other problems that suddenly appear equally important, if not more critical. You're spinning your wheels trying to figure out what to do first.

Stop. Reconsider. Think again. If something does indeed loom larger in importance, choose to fix that and put aside the other ideas for now. If, after reflecting, you still feel the original problem remains the priority, fix that and put all the other ideas in abeyance.

Remember to leave some room for your students' suggestions! They'll love feeling part of their new classroom!

WHO ME?

As anyone who has ever observed children on a playground knows, kids can be bossy. As anyone who has ever worked with other adults knows, they can be bossy too.

With the can-do attitude that many teachers have, sometimes in a burst of exuberance and enthusiasm, the line can get blurry between being cooperative or acting like a leader and being bossy. If you feel yourself dangerously close to the edge of bossy, you can act to:

A. Step back, take a deep breath, and measure your words.
B. Think of how you would feel if you were on the listening end of *you*.
C. Heed your colleagues' input.

BEFORE IT SPIRALS...

Everyone has been there: a meeting that alternates between being positive, tedious, exhilarating, argumentative, enthusiastic, and . . . long.

No matter how much colleagues may respect each other, there are times when someone overdoes it at a meeting, repeatedly saying the same things; getting too personal with others who don't share his or her opinion; going off on a tangent with an individualized, delicate matter that has nothing to do with the meeting or the topics at hand; or just plain hijacking the meeting by talking excessively.

Besides fidgeting, looking away, or sighing, no one knows what to do or say.

When no one is in charge or when the person in charge doesn't do anything to alter the dynamic, what happens?

It should be simple enough to put things back on track by calling on any rules and procedures that are part of your protocol. Sometimes those procedures go by the boards, and no one can remember the last time they were actually used. And no one wants to be responsible for activating them.

That brings us to action versus inaction—and thinking about the advice you would give your students. With that in mind, and in an effort to be proactive, not reactive, perhaps it is time to remind everyone of any rules and procedures that are supposed to guide your meetings.

Maybe there are measures limiting how long someone can talk at one time or a proviso mandating that only matters pertinent to the topic should be discussed. Practices such as these can be straightforward, impartial, and practical alternatives to allowing a meeting to spiral out of hand and cause hard feelings among the participants.

When clear-cut measures aren't in place (maybe a good idea to try to get them launched?), no one is in charge, or the leader is ineffective, it may be left to someone else—perhaps you—to try to put things on an even keel.

Often, no one wants to say anything, but a combination of respect for the speaker and the leader and a big dose of common sense can help. Sometimes people don't realize they're repeating themselves, and sometimes they do so to excessively drive a point home. It might be helpful to ask, "Is there something new you'd like to add?" If the conversation has gone off on a tangent, suggest that the speaker's topic be taken up at a subsequent meeting or at a different meeting with the people it directly affects.

There is always the obvious fact that the meeting has gone on too long and everyone is tired: "Let's continue at another time."

It's always helpful to remember that, at the end of the day, everyone is there for a common purpose: to come together for the good of all the students.

About the Author

Lin Josephson is a former business journalist and first-grade teacher. She is a philosophy for children practitioner, endorsed by the Institute for the Advancement of Philosophy for Children (Montclair State University) and a 2013–2014 recipient of a Philosophy Learning and Teaching Organization Award for excellence in philosophy teaching by a nonclassroom teacher. She is the author of several language arts and science workbooks and has written freelance articles for such publications as *Barron's* and *The Chicago Tribune*. Lin and her husband, Sandy, live "down the shore" in New Jersey.

www.ingramcontent.com/pod-product-compliance
Lightning Source LLC
Chambersburg PA
CBHW032028230426
43671CB00005B/239